EAST OF IPSWICH

Teenage Adventures
in an Antique Land
1979 - 1981

T J MARTIN

Published in the United Kingdom by
T J Martin
4 Fop St. Uley
Dursley
GL11 5AJ

April 2014

ISBN 978-0-9928844-0-6

For Elena & Arthur

CONTENTS

FOREWORD

I was about fourteen when at a scout jumble sale I came across a very tatty paperback copy of an account of the an overland expedition by Land Rover from London to Singapore (and back) and became fascinated by the descriptions of the adventures and challenges faced by the student adventurers back in 1956. I was particularly interested to read about their crossing of the Middle East and of the wild landscapes through which they battled together – the ever-present heat, the dust and the energy sapping humidity they had to cope with as they passed through foreign cultures and ancient civilisations. What stood out for me was that they had taken advantage of every opportunity presented to them. The reason given by the author for undertaking such a mammoth expedition of some 32,000 miles was because he could. I think it was then that I decided an academic future could wait, I wanted to do something different when I left school; I only had to spot the opportunity.

In writing this account of my experiences more than thirty years ago I have had to rely heavily on my memory. I didn't go abroad with the object of recording all that I saw and experienced for later recounting; I was after all setting out on the first steps of adult life and my preoccupation was in experiencing whatever came before me. I felt afterwards that it was impossible to share this experience. Indeed, when I returned to England to commence a degree course at Polytechnic I found it hard to relate to my peers, most of whom had at best inter-railed around Western Europe and at worst arrived straight from school into the "adult" world of higher education; how could they know what it was like to stand in a remote desert for hours waiting hopefully for a lift, or trying to communicate in sign language with someone who knows no English and cannot hear? I kept no copious diaries recording the details of my encounters and deeds, nor did I have vast albums of photographs to illustrate my journeys. I had then, as I have now, the memories of the people and places that I happened upon. Most are indelible in my recollection although some have come back to mind with reference to some meagre notes I made at the time and various documents I have retained, or have been rekindled by current events in parts of the Arab world with which I was familiar. I did however possess a copy of Fodor's "Jordan and the Holy Land" and a 1975 edition of Bartholomew's Mini Atlas – the latter being invaluable in planning my journeys.

There were many instances when arriving at a destination after a day's arduous hitch-hiking I had no funds with which to pay entrance fees to popular antiquities or attractions and had therefore to be content with the knowledge that I had experienced their presence if not their substance! Aqaba, Jerusalem, Cairo, Beirut, Amman, Gaza, Hama, Sharjah, Adana, Damascus – these are not just names to me, but real places with real people. Here I experienced the culture of a fascinating part of the world and whilst still a teenager learned something of its people, politics and history through a series of remarkable adventures while hitch-hiking across deserts and undertaking voluntary work with deaf children.

I worked with those who had dedicated their lives for the benefit of improving the conditions and life chances of those less fortunate than themselves; it was a humbling experience and I am glad to have found that opportunity.

A brief word about the account itself is perhaps helpful. Where it is of interest or helps in the explanation I have included information which I have uncovered from later research. Whilst this is generally historical fact, some of which is contemporary with my own time in the Middle East, I have avoided where at all possible the inclusion of any information which post-dates that time. I have also tried to avoid any comparison with the present day. Readers familiar with this part of the world will immediately make such a comparison, but those who are not may enjoy this account for what it is – an illustration of the formative years of a teenage youth living and travelling in a sometimes volatile land. I made more than one journey to Jordan, initially travelling under the auspices of a charity called The Project Trust by ship from Glasgow. I then spent a year in that country undertaking voluntary work with several short trips to Syria, Israel and Egypt before returning briefly to England by the somewhat mundane means of international air flight (the only excitement on that journey being provided by an unlikely encounter with the actress Olivia Newton John whilst approaching passport control at Heathrow). I made an overland return journey the following year, relying generally on hitch-hiking as a means of transportation supplemented when necessary, or for specific reasons, by public transport. On that occasion I passed through Jordan on the outward and return legs. This account therefore does not easily fall into a chronological sequence, and so I have departed when appropriate from such constraint and endeavoured to group accounts into a more narrative structure. At times I travelled alone, but generally I had a companion – although not always the same one. Consequently references to "we" may not always be references to the same persons.

INTRODUCTION

S ome thirty years ago the region generally known as the Middle East was in many parts quite a different world from today. Although it was common to see four-legged modes of transport around towns and in rural areas, the Mercedes saloon car was already ubiquitous and fast overtaking (in both senses) more traditional means of transport. Tourists were a comparatively rare species and hotels tended to extremes of comfort, such as the Inter-Continental for business-types or doss-houses for migrant workers and occasional back-packers, with little in between. Foreigners were a novelty, seen as fair game for the local population to practice their English language skills upon rather than as a walking wallet or someone to be exploited. There was a sense of naivety of the ways of the western Europeans and an inclination to share local ways and customs rather than to adopt a more European way of doing things. In downtown Amman the numerous small stalls selling music in compact cassette format (nearly always of a boot-leg variety with labels neatly hand written perhaps indicating home recording by the vendor) offered only Middle Eastern performers – Fairuz the popular Lebanese singer being a hot favourite. The inevitable part completed concrete homes with reinforcement ironwork poking out like radio aerials from the tops of rough concrete columns symbolised either a ploy to avoid paying building tax or a temporary setback in securing the funds to continue with the work, and not an indicator of global economic growth or recession.

It was barely thirty years since the countries of Jordan, Syria, Israel and Lebanon had all finally become independent nations. They had been at war with each other on and of ever since: Israel with Egypt and Syria in 1948; Israel with Egypt, Syria & Jordan in 1967 (in which Jordan lost the West Bank and Jerusalem); Syria with Jordan in 1970; Jordan with Palestinian guerrillas in 1971; Israel with Egypt, Syria & Jordan again in 1973; Lebanon with itself and variously with Israel and Syria from 1976.

Between 1979 and 1981 war did not seem very far away either. Russia invaded Afghanistan; Iraq invaded Iran soon after Saddam Hussein came to power and Ayatollah Khomeini returned from exile; North and South Yemen took up cudgels against each other; Israel annexed the Golan Heights and the US embassy staff in Tehran were being held hostage. Not content with American hostages and attacks on Saddam's forces, the Iranians also started an offensive against the Kurds. Meanwhile the Israelis found time to destroy an alleged Iraqi plutonium production facility. There were some notable executions and massacres as well, with President Bhutto being executed in Pakistan; Muslims killing Christians in Cairo;

Anwar Sadat the Egyptian president shot – to be replaced by Hosni Mubarak. Tariq Aziz the Iraqi vice-premier survived an attempted assassination, a good fortune he was also to share with President Hafez al-Assad of Syria.

Eastern Europe too was very different from what it is today, with travel behind the "Iron Curtain" into communist territory a mysterious and somewhat unnerving adventure in itself. There was no early indication of the impending break up of communism in these countries and that the balance of world power would shift, nor that there would be a rise in the influence of Islamic inspired groups worldwide.

I knew no-one who had ever travelled to these parts and learning as I did that I was to be sent to work in Jordan only a few days before I set sail, I had little time to research the country and the region generally. I learned that there was currently a volunteer working in the school where I was going, but that I would not have the benefit of meeting him before I arrived to take over. In short, I was leaping into the unknown.

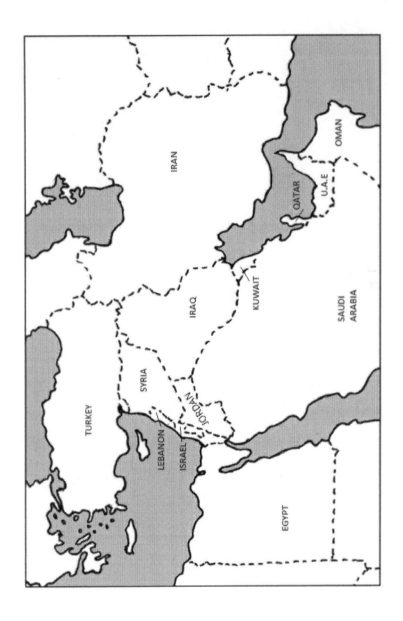

Map of the Middle East in 1980

1

ISLE OF COLL

"...all experience is an arch wherethro' gleams that untravell'd world..."

Alfred Tennyson – Ulysses, 1842

So this was the Hebrides. After a seriously long train journey from Ipswich I had taken the early morning Caledonian MacBrayne ferry from Oban and arrived at Arinagour on Coll with the rain not falling in sheets but flying horizontally on a very cold March morning in 1979. I was not alone, there were a number of similarly uncertain looking seventeen and eighteen year olds disembarking with me; we were about to undergo four days assessment on the island with the hope of being selected as volunteers to be sent overseas by the Project Trust, a charity with its headquarters on this treeless rock. We'd nearly all heard from someone who had been through the experience previously what we might expect; a billet in a damp castle; interrogation by a mad Major in a kilt; hard labour on the croft; enforced listening to bagpipes! In the end we were to find all these unsettling stories to be true with the exception of the billet – we were each to be farmed out to obliging crofters who arranged with the Major to provide bed and breakfast for a steady stream of would-be volunteers during the assessment weeks on the island.

As we gathered together in a rather soggy huddle on the quay a Land Rover pulled up. Here was our lift to the castle I thought. Out jumped a brusque and healthy-looking type in my opinion somewhat unsuitably dressed in a just a woolly jumper and a kilt. After a brief word of welcome in a very upper-class military voice the Major (as he wished to be known) loaded our rucksacks into the back and turned to me (being the tallest I think I was the most visible) and cracked what was to be the first order of the week: "Take this map! You are here" he pointed to a rather soggy point on the ancient OS map, "You have to get to here" again he pointed, "Oh, and lunch is at thirteen hundred hours, so don't be late!" Then he left us. We estimated it was more than six miles to the unpronounceable Breacach-adh Castle and there were some among us who had left water-proofs in their rucksacks…. happily I was not one. We made haste as best we could, bent almost double against the wind. By this time I swore that the rain was blowing upwards as I was soaked from below as well as above. Finally we made it to a bleak looking 15th century stone castle on the edge of a promontory from where the Major was to beckon us standing at the top of an open stone staircase one storey up the castle's flank, his kilt flying precariously.

Project Trust was, and is, an educational charity set up by the Major (Major Nicholas Maclean-Bristol OBE) in 1968 while on secondment from the British army. Its aim was to educate a new generation and it was not to be an aid organisation. Its first volunteers were sent to Ethiopia.

This island had been used by the Major and his wife Lavinia as a selection centre for nearly ten years. It was to serve as a model by which volunteers could learn how a different community worked and would simulate many of the challenges we were to face overseas. The selection course was run very much on military lines and unbeknown to us our hosts with whom we were billeted would provide useful intelligence to help with our selection. This meant that anyone who visited the one bar in the hotel by the quay after an arduous day of interviews and presentations would be sure to be reported; and any moaning about aching backs and lack of sleep would be frowned upon. We all knew that a small number of us would not be considered suitable to be sent overseas as volunteers and so there was competitive element to everything we did and scant understanding that it was all about character and attitude.

Over the course of the four days I recall my guard being dropped several times – I guess that was part of the plan – and in common with others I had no idea whether I had sufficiently impressed the "recruiters". An ill-judged attempt at a wise-crack on the first morning left me sure I had blown my chances. We were paired up and set the task of finding out as much as possible about our partner as we could. As luck would have it I was paired with someone who had very generously lent me the spare bunk in their cabin the night before we sailed from Oban, thus giving me ample opportunity to find out all about them and their aspirations over a glass or two of the local malt. Without really thinking, I ended my assessment with the throw-away comment "Oh, and she snores dreadfully in her sleep". There must have been a full ten seconds of silence during which I looked desperately about me for a suitably sized hole to swallow me up before the Major passed on without comment to the next pair.

Throughout our stay there were presentations to give on what we had learned of island culture and team building exercises both in the classroom and out on the croft. The latter consisting of going down to the beautiful sandy foreshore near the castle to collect seaweed and sand to bring up to the "lazy-beds" for digging in to help with the formation of a meagre topsoil. This work was quite literally back breaking and I ended that day so stiff that it was only with a great deal of difficulty that I could extricate myself from the bath that evening and bring myself to get ready for what was trailed as "an evening of traditional entertainment" a euphemism we thought for the enforced bag-pipe performance by the Major's young son that we had been warned about. In the event it turned out to be a *ceilidh* – with bagpipes. It was probably the highlight of the week for most of us, though not for the reason originally intended; that of a chance to relax and spend some time socialising. During the course of one particularly enthusiastic interpretation of "strip-the-willow" one of our number was accidentally hurled by the Major's wife into the ancient hearth in the centre of the great hall where enormous peat fire was attempting to keep us warm. It was to his credit that he restrained himself from apportioning any blame for the sprained ankle he suffered – no doubt conscious that no decisions would yet have been made on selections.

Soon enough, our time on Coll was over and we departed, along with the rain, on the same ferry which had brought us from Oban and would no doubt be bringing a fresh batch of unsuspecting victims the following week. Most of us were to meet again in a few weeks, with arms still aching from smallpox and cholera jabs, for a briefing prior to despatch to all quarters of the globe: Hong Kong; Australia; Argentina; South Africa, India, Kenya, Egypt and Jordan.

I was to be sent to work at a school for deaf children in a small hill-town called Salt in Jordan, although I was not to learn my destination until a few days before my departure.

2

ALL AT SEA

"A ship is floating in the harbour now,
A wind is hovering o'er the mountain's brow;
There is a path on the sea's azure floor,
No keel has ever ploughed that path before;..."

Percy Bysshe Shelley - Epipsychidion, 1821

I awoke to find myself in what appeared to be a coffin. It was pitch black and my head was thumping. Whenever I moved my arms they struck the hard wooden sides of the box I was lying in, something was restricting the movement of my legs and for some inexplicable reason I was rolling from side to side. Nearby, above the throbbing of a powerful engine I could hear someone apparently kicking a dustbin; I had to find a way to stop him from making the pain in my head worse. The engine seemed to be running at full speed with its leaky exhaust pipe forcing fumes into the already stuffy room. I struggled to get up but the sides of the box were stopping me, the whole room seemed to be swaying and I wasn't sure I really wanted to move anyway. Slowly though, I came to from my sleep and realised that there was someone knocking on the metal door. Clearly I had a serious hang-over and my inclination was not to investigate and to stay exactly where I was - a tactic which had always proved effective on previous occasions, but as the banging persisted it became clear that it wasn't going to work this time and I'd have to brave it and get up and stop whoever was making that awful noise. As I made a second attempt to escape what I discovered was a bunk, a very small man entered the room and quietly placed a cup of tea on the locker by my head. From close to he appeared to be of Indian origin, but it was still dark and before I could make any comment or offer any thanks he had slipped out. Slowly as I sipped the lukewarm sickly liquid (made with condensed milk I was sure) I began to feel more human and after several large gulps started to take in my surroundings.

I was in a small cabin somewhere at sea as the pitching movement indicated; the throbbing noise and the fumes must have been coming from the ship's engines somewhere below me. This was in the Irish Sea – I'd left Glasgow sometime in the night – my last memory was of sitting on a barstool in the ship's saloon downing a succession of large glasses of Southern Comfort with some of the ship's officers who were to be my companions for the next fortnight or so. It felt like the first step of an odyssey. I wasn't behind the wheel of a Land Rover... but then I wasn't sitting squashed in an airline economy seat either, like most of my fellow volunteers embarking on their first year away from home. This adventure was just the prelude. Suddenly I realised I must get up – there was a whole ship to explore, and so I made my way only slightly gingerly back to the officer's mess.

The voyage began at the King George V dock on the Clyde where the ship had been tied up for a day or two collecting the final part of its mixed cargo; cases of Johnnie Walker whiskey and Tennent's Lager. I'd been assigned the job with two of the ship's cadets, of ensuring that the Glaswegian stevedores didn't steal *too much* whiskey - what they thought a skinny eighteen year old would do to stop such a burly workforce I had no idea. After climbing down into the hold to obtain a better view of proceedings I simply plonked myself down on the nearest pallet of cardboard cases, which had just that minute been deposited from the end of a long cable controlled by some unseen crane driver, to watch the Glaswegian stevedores guide the cargo into the hold – and promptly sank up to my armpits. The cases I'd chosen for my seat, although apparently sealed, were completely empty! Clearly I needed to be more observant; so I prodded several nearby cases until I eventually found one solid enough to provide a more suitable perch from where to watch the best conjuring act I'd seen to date. After a while I had worked out what was going on; the trick was quite blatant really, it relied not on sleight of hand or misdirection, but on enormous beer bellies and the dexterity of the man sat with his legs over the edge of the hold directing the crane driver with hand signals. Occasionally an unbalanced case would topple from a pallet as it moved into position in the hold and one stevedore would then open the case to see if there were any breakages – which there never seemed to be – he'd then quickly throw one bottle after another straight up to his partner sitting on the edge of the hold who would immediately throw them over his shoulder to an accomplice without interrupting his direction of the crane. Any which remained in the "damaged" case were stuffed into trouser belts and covered up by baggy jumpers, totally concealed by already bulging bellies. Clearly these were professionals, and my NFPP (Non Fare-Paying Passenger) status didn't require me to undertake heroics. I made a quick assessment of what might constitute "too much" and decided the threshold had not been reached, there being some 50,000 cases already loaded, and settled down to watch the entertainment. I learned that the stevedores were working on four hour shifts – I presumed that this equated with the time it took for each man to become incapable due to drink. Fortunately the man operating the crane must have been teetotal as he managed to deposit each pallet into the hold with unerring accuracy.

The ship I had joined was the Clan Graham; a 9,308 ton freighter built in 1962 and owned by the Clan Line. A company which I discovered had a distinguished history, being formed from the Cayzer Irvine Company which apparently had been the largest cargo carrying concern in the world as recently as the 1930s (they must have been sizable as they lost 30 ships in World War II). With the coming of container shipping however, the parent company British & Commonwealth Shipping was in the process of diversifying into a financial services company. My journey must have been one of the last voyages of the Clan Graham, as the Clan Line was to cease trading in 1981 whereupon the ship was sold to the Panamanians and renamed Candelaria. The ship's company comprised about sixteen officers, mainly Scottish, and an unspecified number of Bangladeshi crew plus two cadets. They were setting out on a seven month voyage by way of the Suez Canal to Bangladesh. The ship would be putting in to Aqaba, Aden, Mombasa, Bombay and Mauritius to unload its cargo before sailing on to Chittagong to change crew and thence return to Glasgow. My ride was only as far as the first port of call, Aqaba in Jordan, which we would apparently reach in fifteen days.

It soon became clear to me that an NFPP had a special status aboard ship. Being strictly a passenger I was not required to work and was assigned a steward who brought me morning tea in my cabin, I also had a table to myself in the officer's mess. Furthermore, I was to discover later, that I was allowed to drink "shorts" at the bar – whereas junior officers and cadets were restricted to lager while at sea. Luckily I only discovered this just as I was leaving ship, what with lager at 16p a pint and whiskey at only 4p a shot (Scottish measures) I might have had more hangovers, something I had no desire to repeat after my experience that first morning in the Irish Sea. Wanting to quickly integrate with my fellow sailors I joined forces with the cadets and thereafter was assigned to share their duties, which seemed to mainly comprise taking regular temperature readings of the double-bottom tanks; an intriguing name for the void below the hold between the hold bottom and the steel hull. A thermometer on a very long cord was lowered into a small pipe through the deck and the temperatures were recorded regularly at various locations; any increase in temperature would indicate an outbreak of fire in the hold. The other vital task I performed was the recording of serial numbers on the steel blocks and shackles attached to the derricks. The crew would shin up the derricks and lower the blocks individually for us to clean down with a wire brush and then log the number against the appropriate safety certificate. It seemed that Indian port officials were noted for their ingenuity in finding reasons to extract a fine from visiting ships, and not being able to produce on demand a certificate matched to a particular block or shackle was an important income opportunity not to be passed up by any enterprising safety inspector. I was assured that another task absolutely vital to the safety of the ship was the need for an up-to-date paint inventory.

We were passing through the Bay of Biscay, a notoriously choppy area of sea, when I was asked to report to the forward locker where the cadets were about to commence preparation of the inventory. Whilst I didn't normally suffer from sea-sickness, having spent my early childhood on an island and spent much time in small boats, the combination of the pitching of the ship so far towards the bow and the oily smells emanating from the store left me rather queasy. It was of course a point of honour not to display any discomfort to the seasoned cadets and so I duly descended the iron rungs of the bulkhead ladder down into the store beneath and thence again down into what was by now an unlit triangular cavern in the bows of the ship several feet below the deck. The only light being that which was lowered down on a rope by a helpful cadet, I could see little but could hear water sloshing around immediately below me and then I realised that the compartment below was flooded as ballast and I was in fact many feet below the waterline. The thump of each wave as the bow cut through the sea appeared to come from somewhere above my head. Here I was to open each tin of paint to inspect its colour and record this on the inventory. I started to smell a rat; indeed it was far more than a rat I could smell – as the fumes were soon overpowering. Suddenly the light was hauled up on its rope and the hatch banged shut with two laughing cadets standing on top! For anyone suffering from even the mildest claustrophobia this would have been a nightmare. Luckily my desire to express my personal feelings towards my tormentors in a loud and colourful manner proved a distraction. It was only afterwards, once the joke's humorous impact had apparently worn off and I was released, that I succumbed and went wobbly at the knees. It seemed however that I was now accepted as a true seaman! I was thankful that I wasn't staying with the ship until Mombassa and so have to suffer the indignities imposed by Poseidon as an initiate crossing the equator for the first time.

The days passed all too quickly. A routine was soon established with the previous evening's meal becoming the basis for the following day's lunchtime curry. I had my own steward at mealtimes (as befitted my status!) so these were a rather solitary affair; socialising being deferred until evening when all the officers seemed to congregate in the saloon or mess as it was known. Much to my surprise this was without a steward, perhaps through some religious objection the Bangladeshi crew would not serve alcohol. The arrangement was to simply write one's order in an old school exercise book and settle one's mess bill at the end of the voyage. With a round of beers or spirits costing little over £1 for the entire company I could afford to be generous. Somehow I still managed to accrue a mess bill in excess of £20 by the time I disembarked, though through the generosity of the first mate I was allowed to reduce this to nothing in a hard-fought battle of Chinese chequers on my final evening in the mess. We were allowed to buy, again on credit, 200 cigarettes out of bond every week. At the time I was strictly a "roll-up" smoker but was nevertheless persuaded to take out my quota so that others might win them off me at darts games in the mess and so augment their apparently meagre allowance. It was about this time that I started to grow a beard, or rather side-burns, as they didn't really join up in the middle. This wasn't through choice (as I had acquired a brand new electric razor just before departure) but out of necessity upon discovering that the ship's electrical supply was direct current and not compatible with my alternating current electric razor. I never did use that razor and as I eschewed a wet shave I went shaggy ever after, happily in due course the side-burns did join up.

We passed through the Straits of Gibraltar at night and I was allowed onto the bridge to watch the scores of ships passing each way through the straits on the radar screen, rather like being in the control tower at Heathrow I imagined. As we passed through into the Mediterranean the weather became noticeably warmer, it was August and the officers changed to "whites" and with our lunchtime curry came our daily ration of anti-malarial tablets. Flying fish could be seen swimming alongside and the occasional porpoise sent me running for my camera – the photographic results I subsequently discovered being somewhat less impressive than the real thing.

The Chief Engineer's offer of a tour of the engine room was certainly a highlight of the voyage. I was not prepared for the noise; almost unbeara-ble even with ear protection. When invited to lie against the sloping stern bulkhead underneath the propeller shaft I had no hesitation in accepting the offer. "Not many people will have done this I thought?" as I watched the foot-wide steel shaft spinning rapidly just six inches from my face as it disappeared through the steel plate to join a presumably massive propeller just on the other side. "You're nearly ninety feet below the deck now" I was told.....suddenly I had a great desire to see the horizon again.

Sailing eastwards every day we soon came within sight of the coast of Algeria which was the first land I had seen since leaving the dockside at

Glasgow. Shortly we arrived at the port of Suez and anchored just outside the harbour to await the next convoy going through the canal. Entertainment was provided for us by the porpoises showing off in the water all around us and the hectic activity of Egyptians in small boats circling and clamouring to be allowed on board to sell their goods. Suddenly an unseen signal was given and we were off, line astern in a convoy of some half dozen ships of which only those immediately in front and behind were clearly visible. As we passed the Suez Canal Defence Monument I realised how narrow this water way was and that it had been fought over several times in its history. The monument had been designed by French architects and built to commemorate the allied defence of the canal against the Turks in World War I. The two colossal figures of *"Serene Intelligence"* and *"Serene Force"* seated at its base were just visible from the ship's deck.

How strange to be sailing through a desert, I could almost feel that I had arrived at the start of my Arabian adventure – perhaps on a "ship of the desert" (there were many of them to be seen on both sides of us as we steamed through towards the Bitter Lakes). Located at about the half way point these formed a passing place for the north travelling ships while we carried on in our south-bound convoy until finally leaving the canal at Port Said. A sharp change of direction to port and we were sailing up the western coast of Saudi Arabia with the Sinai Peninsula on our port side. Occasionally I could see clusters of white buildings indicating littoral settlements at the foot of barren mountains to the east, these glowed orange and purple as the evening sun reflected off their slopes. All too soon the land could be seen on all three sides of us and I realised we had reached Aqaba our first port of call and time for me to make my farewells to the ship's company. Over the bows of the ship I could see the Israeli town of Eilat merging into the Jordanian township. There was a small wharf at the port but this was reserved solely for cement and phosphate ships; the practice for cargo ships was to unload onto pontoons towed out by the Jordanian dock workers. While this was being arranged I said my good-byes and waited to learn how I was to disembark. By mid morning a customs and immigration launch had arrived and I was visited in my cabin and asked to fill in various forms regarding my luggage which was then diligently searched. After stamping my visa the officials promptly departed, whereupon my cabin suddenly filled with half the ship's company bringing gifts of cigarette cartons and other goodies they assured me would be absolutely vital for my survival – like penknives and dope pipes! It seemed they had sent a message to the shipping agent asking for a launch to now come and take me off the ship and ensure I was pointed in the right direction for the next part of my journey.

Very shortly, with my rucksack and overweight steel trunk, I was set down with great informality on the wharf. I realised I had arrived and would now have to start to rely on my own wits. A hot flush of panic hit me, it was either that or the dry searing wind blowing down from the hills that lined the shore, but I had no time to contemplate – there were no more formalities to be got through and I duly found myself the last passenger to be squashed into the back of a beaten up old Mercedes shared taxi (called *servees taxi* locally) full of chain-smoking old men, winding its way up a very steep road through bare limestone hills towards the Desert Highway and onto my ultimate destination the unknown town of Salt. Not for the first time did I wonder what I'd signed up for.

3

THE HASHEMITE KINGDOM OF JORDAN

"....I could not conceive of a small country having so large a history."

Mark Twain - The Innocents Abroad, 1869

Jordan was a country almost completely unknown to me except that I was aware that it was ruled by a King who had been to the Royal Military Academy at Sandhurst and that it was a land containing a lot of sand but no oil, but nothing much more had hitherto come to my attention. It wasn't in my geography curriculum at school so consequently it could have been of little importance or we should have learned about its contribution to the world economy or its amazing glacial features..... Unlike the Lebanon, it had not been on the television news almost nightly with film of smoking buildings and stories of Christian and Muslim fighting. I knew it adjoined Israel and had been involved in various wars in my lifetime and was currently at peace, but I had no real idea of its geography or history. It seemed that all I really knew of the country could be found in the traditional song "Swing Low Sweet Chariot"; Eric Clapton's version being on one of the few cassettes I had brought with me, the lyrics of which contained doubtful information regarding the presence of angels. I thought it best to balance this authority by also taking a copy of the music by a band called America: "Horse with No Name" – with its tale of riding through the desert and being out of the rain. One or other was certain to capture the essence of the place. Just to be sure, I also took a few taped copies of my Camel albums, probably more to remind me of friends left behind at home, but nevertheless part of the essential kit of an intrepid desert explorer. There was no time to read "Seven Pillars of Wisdom" nor tales of Wilfred Thesinger's desert explorations before I joined my ship in Glasgow. At the Project Trust briefing a few weeks before departure all the other volunteers had been given a copy of a report on their particular project written by an earlier returned volunteer, but I was offered only the palliative "Nobody has yet come back from Jordan so we can't properly brief you." I wasn't going to repeat this to my parents, lest they thought that I had deliberately omitted the word "alive" from the sentence. Secretly of course I was very excited at the prospect of being a true explorer; at least until the first volunteer at my project had returned to the UK and reported back to the Major. Until then I was apparently heading into the unknown.

I acquired sparse and arguably partial information about the country from the Jordanian embassy in London when I went to obtain my visa:

"Jordan is a developing Arab country formed of the East Bank and West Bank of the Jordan River. The East Bank constitutes what was formerly known as the Emirate of Trans-Jordan established in

1921 and proclaimed "The Hashemite Kingdom of Jordan" after achieving independence in 1946. The West Bank is that part of Palestine, excluding the Gaza Strip, which the Arabs were able to save during the Arab - Israeli war in 1948. Unity between the two Banks came into being in 1950. However, the West Bank fell under Israeli occupation in 1967.

Jordan is situated off the south eastern shores of the Mediterranean (between longitudes 34° and 39° East and latitudes 29° and 33° North) and extends eastwards into the Arabian Desert. It has a total area of 96,188 square kilometres of which the West Bank forms an enclave of 6,633 square kilometres.

The population was estimated in 1972 at 2,467,000 of whom 720,000 live in the West Bank. Population growth is 3.2 per cent. Jordan is a constitutional monarchy. King Abdullah, the grandfather of the present Monarch, King Hussein, was the founder of the Hashemite dynasty, in Jordan. Under the Constitution the King is vested with wide powers which he exercises through the Prime Minister and the Council of Ministers. Legislative power resides in the National Assembly consisting of the Senate and the House of Deputies.

Jordan has suffered repeatedly from the conflict and upheaval that has beset the Middle East since World War 1. In spite of this, the country has attempted to utilize, to the best of its ability, its human and natural resources through economic and social development programmes. Although the Kingdom received a severe setback as a result of the fighting and occupation of the West Bank in 1967, Jordan as of 1973 launched the three year development plan 1973-1975 with the overall objective of reactivating the national economy and resuming the developmental momentum witnessed prior to 1967."

The Ministry had also helpfully published a booklet on the country's agriculture and livestock production which it appeared occupied some 40% of the total workforce. The land apparently fell into four main physiographic regions: the Jordan Valley, the highland, the steppe and the

---

* Ministry of Culture and Information 1975

desert, with significantly different variations in climate in each of these areas. The Jordan Valley was perhaps the best known feature; a giant trough traversing the country longitudinally, with mountain ranges for sides; the northern-most extension of the Great African Rift Valley, the other end of which was some 2,500 miles further south. The rift or trough could be followed as far south as Lake Tanganyika in Tanzania, but this northerly section was comparatively narrow and incredibly deep.

The northern segment of the Jordan Valley is the country's most fertile region. It contains the Jordan River and extends from the northern border down to the Dead Sea. The Jordan River rises from several sources, mainly the Anti-Lebanon Mountains in Syria, and flows down into Lake Tiberias (the Sea of Galilee). It then drains into the Dead Sea where it is less than 100ft wide near its endpoint. To the south lie Wadi Araba and then the coastal town of Aqaba and the Red Sea. The Jordan Valley has influenced human life for thousands of years by providing fertile lowland and a warm, wet semi-tropical region of luxurious vegetation. In Roman times Jericho, sited near the delta of the River Jordan, was described as the most fertile spot in Judea. At the valley's lowest point, nearly 1,400 ft below sea level, lies the Dead Sea whose surface has been lowering and shrinking in extent continuously due to water extraction along the course of the River Jordan. Salt concentration in the Dead Sea fluctuates at around 31% making the water extremely dense (about one and a quarter kilos per litre) and not only useless for irrigation, but for swimming too; although floating can be most relaxing - unless the surface has been disturbed by recent stormy weather and waves are rolling onto the shore, in which case a form of body-surfing can be practiced as I was able to confirm on my first visit to its shores. The climate can be oppressive here, with increased atmospheric pressure and high temperatures – averaging around 70°F in winter and up to 100°F in the summer. Interestingly, Britain obtained half of its potash supplies from here during World War II. Supplies were extracted by the Palestine Potash Company founded in 1929, at plants located at Kalya and Sodom (on the western and southern shores) which were then sent by truck to Jerusalem and on to the port of Haifa. Potash was not just used as a crop fertiliser but was an important constituent of black powder used in armament manufacture. Germany had plentiful supplies from mines near Carlsbad and was the sole supplier to America until the outbreak of World War I when they were briefly interrupted, subsequently continuing right up to 1939, when fortunately for both the Americans and the British new resources were discovered in New Mexico.

The highlands of Jordan, comprising the uplands to the east of the Jordan Valley, receive Jordan's highest rainfall and rise to an average height of 3,000 ft and up to 5,400 ft. They separate the Jordan Valley and its margins from the plains of the eastern desert. This region extends the entire length of the western part of the country, hosting most of Jordan's main population centres and providing the most richly vegetated areas. Intersected by a number of valleys and riverbeds known as *wadis*, all of which eventually flow into the Jordan River, the Dead Sea or the usually-dry Wadi Araba, the northern part of the mountain heights plateau known as the northern highlands extends southwards to just north of the capital Amman and has a typical Mediterranean climate and vegetation. This region was known historically as the Land of Gilead.

South and east of the northern highlands are the northern steppes, which serve as a buffer between the highlands and the eastern desert. This area was formerly covered in steppe vegetation of which much has been lost to desertification. This high altitude plain receives little annual rainfall and is consequently lightly vegetated.

Desert comprises around 75% of Jordan and is known as the North Arab Desert which stretches into Syria, Iraq and Saudi Arabia, with elevations varying between 1,900ft and 2,900ft above sea level. Climate varies widely between day and night, and between summer and winter. Daytime summer temperatures can exceed 104°F, while winter nights can be very cold, dry and windy. Vegetation types vary considerably according to their underlying geology; which is volcanic and black boulder strewn in the north in the area bordering Syria, undulating limestone to the east, while to the south in the Wadi Rum region the desert is more sandy, and is dominated by towering sandstone outcrops.

Tourism played a small part in the Jordan's economy at this time. Whilst the country was well endowed with a wealth of religious sites and antiquities, little investment had been made in infrastructure which might have encouraged foreign visitors to such sites as Jerash, Kerak, Petra and the Dead Sea. Tourists were a rarity, perhaps finding the political situation generally in the Middle East off-putting. So much so that when in December 1978 a group of 400 American tourists arrived on a four-day visit this event was reported in the national newspaper.

Unsurprisingly, given the geography and history of the country, the population in 1979 of just fewer than 3,000,000 (if the 700,000 or so in the West Bank were included) comprised a variety of ethnic or religious groups, the largest being predominantly Arab in origin and Sunni Muslim in religion, this being the orthodox branch of Islam. Circassians also existed as a distinctly ethnic group being Sunni Muslims from the Caucasus. Only about 7% of the population was Christian. The largest population group, comprising about 40%, were Palestinian refugees from the wars of 1948 and 1967. Another 30% were residents of what was formerly Trans-Jordan and only about 11% nomadic or semi-nomadic Bedouin. Very few of the latter remained truly nomadic (less than 5%) and a University of Jordan survey of 1978 showed that the Bedouin were the worst off group by all measures including education, health and housing with child mortality rates more than 60% higher than the East Bank average. Poor management of the sparse pastures to the east of the Desert Highway upon which they depended for their goats, sheep and camels meant that they were gravitating to the towns in ever increasing numbers. The greatest influx of Circassians came in the late nineteenth century and consisted of several small but significant groups. They had two seats allotted in the Jordanian Parliament and several senior ranking government and military officials came from their number. Various minority groups existed, with Christians being the largest, comprising Greek Orthodox, Catholic, Protestant and Armenian.

Many of the largest single group of people, the Palestinians, lived in large numbers in ten refugee camps, four of which had been in existence since 1949. Although given immediate citizenship by the Jordanian government they were administered by UNRWA (United Nations Relief and Works Agency). This Agency, which still provides assistance, protection and advocacy for nearly 5,000,000 Palestinian refugees of whom nearly 1,500,000 live in fifty-eight recognised camps in the region, was established in 1949 and is funded almost entirely by voluntary contributions from United Nations member states. Without a solution to the Palestinian refugee problem UNRWA, which was originally envisaged as a temporary organisation to look after about 750,000 refugees, has had its mandate continually extended. Descendents of the original refugees are also eligible for registration so it's hard to see how this number can reduce. Several of the children attending the Holy Land Institute for the Deaf came from families living in such camps.

By 1979 some twelve years had passed since the West Bank region of Jordan had passed into Israeli control, but those in the government ministries responsible for producing maps of the country continued to include it in defiance. After all, a map could still make a strong political statement.

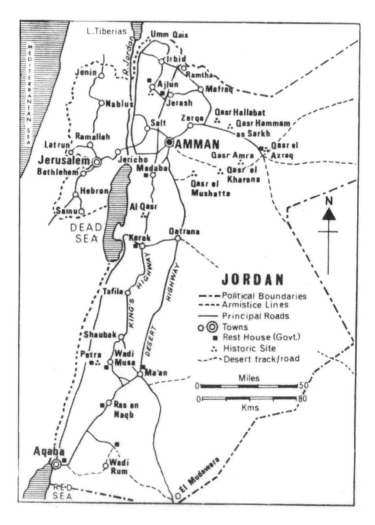

Source: Ministry of Culture & Information, 1975

4

CREATION OF THE MIDDLE EAST

"The futility – not to mention the danger – of Balfour's messing himself up with things between Arabs and Jews is beyond castigation. There's bound to be unnecessary trouble there – before long.

Rudyard Kipling - Letter to Rider Haggard, 1925

The history of the area comprising lands bounded by the Mediterranean in the west, the Tigris and Euphrates in the east, the Taurus Mountains in the north and the Red Sea to the south is long and colourful. To provide either a brief or simple history of the creation of what is the modern Middle East it is necessary to omit great detail on negotiations and manoeuvrings between the British, French and Americans as well as the Arabs and the Zionists in the build up to and the conduct of the Paris Peace negotiations which culminated in the Treaty of Versailles at the end of World War I. Much has been written by historians analysing the emergence of Arab, Jewish and Turkish societies in particular the complex events between 1914 and 1923 including the Great Arab Revolt of 1916, in which several European nations attempted to fulfil their own often selfish ambitions. There were notable individuals who were motivated to establish stability in the region for apparently more altruistic reasons; after all this was one of the goals of the League of Nations which was set up after the war, but often their interventions served only to further complicate or delay the process. Both Britain and France still had pretensions of greatness, having emerged victorious from the war but yet to realise that the age of empires was fast disappearing and that international politics called for less arrogance than had hitherto been the rule. A transformed Middle East was a product of the European wartime rivalries and the inspiration and ability of key individuals to identify and exploit opportunities for the benefit of their people. As ever, the British had a significant hand in the ensuing confusion and difficulties and decisions taken almost 100 years ago still shape both the geography and the politics of the region today.

I have endeavoured to provide a much simplified history in an attempt to outline the complexity behind the origins of the present states and to perhaps throw some light onto some of the reasons for continuing unrests. It is intended to give background to some of the scenes and events I witnessed in my short time in the region. A reader without some basic knowledge of the region's history may fail to empathise with the excitement I felt at being given the opportunity to become immersed within it.

THE OTTOMANS: The area had been under the rule of the Ottomans for some considerable time and formed part of the Ottoman Empire which extended down into what is now Saudi Arabia, but upon the formal ending of hostilities with the British in 1918 this area was under British control, with Sir Edmund Allenby becoming the most powerful man in the Middle

East. His army of more than 1,000,000 men, made up of troops from across the Empire, occupied Jerusalem, Baghdad and Damascus; Egypt was already occupied by that time as a British protectorate.

THE ARABS AND THE ZIONISTS: During the course of the war General Allenby had been fighting the Turks while T. E. Lawrence had sought to unite Arabs under the Hashemite Hussein in a revolt against their occupiers.[*]   Hussein was over 60 at the start of the conflict and Feisal, one of his four sons (three of whom became kings of successor states to the Ottoman Empire), played a key role in both the military and political arenas.   Lawrence made Feisal a promise of British support for an Arab nation following the inevitable defeat of the Ottomans.   Meanwhile, the politicians at home had been keeping a close interest in the situation with an eye to gaining future control for the British and had been making their own plans.   Both the British and their French allies had their eye on a post-war carve-up.

Also lobbying the British and making plans as were the Zionists; who were anxious to seek a Jewish National Home in Palestine as a homeland for Palestinian Jews and a place for immigration of Jews from the many states around Europe where they were suffering various degrees of persecution.   The leader of the Zionist movement was Chaim Weizmann who had supporters both in Europe and the United States as well as amongst prominent Jews in the British Parliament.

Nothing was going to be straightforward for the emerging nations of the Middle East, for the British had made many promises during the course of the war and both Arabs and Jews had high expectations of their own.

SYKES-PICOT AGREEMENT: Britain had made a secret agreement in 1916 with the French in expectation of the downfall of the Ottoman Empire, which became known as the Sykes-Picot Agreement.   In it they divided up the Turkish lands outside of the Arabian peninsula into areas of British and French influence.   Britain was allocated control of areas roughly comprising a coastal strip between the sea and the River Jordan,

---

[*] The traditional homeland for the Hashemites was in what is now Iraq and Saudi Arabia, but they were keen to increase their influence in the area known as Syria and Palestine. Hussein's branch of the Hashemite family, had as "Sharifs" or nobles, ruled the Hejaz in western Arabia for over a thousand years and in particular had ruled over Mecca from 1201 AD to 1925 AD (whilst recognising the sovereignty of the Ottoman sultan in 1517). They were direct descendents of the Prophet Muhammad through the eldest son, Al-Hassan, of his daughter Fatima and her husband Ali bin Abi Talib.

southern Iraq, and a small area including the ports of Haifa and Acre. France was allocated control of south-eastern Turkey, northern Iraq, Syria and Lebanon. Both countries were left free to decide on state boundaries within these areas. This agreement was to be one of the key causes of difficulty for the emerging Middle Eastern states. The other was a declaration made by Arthur Balfour in a letter to Lord Rothschild in 1917. Given Balfour had been the president of the Society for Psychical Research one might have thought that he should have foreseen the ensuing problems; precognition being one of the areas targeted for research by the Society.

THE BALFOUR DECLARATION: In 1916 the great Liberal David Lloyd George became British prime minister and leader of a coalition government, he appointed Arthur Balfour, a former Conservative prime minister, as his foreign secretary. At the time Walter Rothschild, son of the rich Jewish financier Nathan Rothschild and himself a committed Zionist was good friends with Chaim Weizmann. Weizmann had found out about the existence of the Sykes-Picot Agreement which ran counter to Zionist hopes for a British protectorate, and having worked closely with Rothschild to produce a draft declaration for a Jewish homeland in Palestine was anxious to enter negotiations with Balfour to secure a declaration in support of the Zionist cause. He also enlisted the support of the large American Jewish community whose leader at the time had the ear of President Woodrow Wilson. To some extent it was to avoid the intervention of the Americans in the Middle East that the British government was keen to issue a statement of support for Zionism, so when Weizmann wrote to the foreign office seeking such support they were receptive. Negotiations on the draft ensued and it was eventually agreed on 2nd November 1917 whereupon Balfour wrote to Rothschild in a letter subsequently published in the British Press:-

> *"His Majesty's Government view with favour the establishment in Palestine of a national home for the Jewish people, and will use its best endeavours to facilitate the achievement of this object, it being clearly understood that nothing shall be done which may prejudice the civil and religious rights of existing non-Jewish communities in Palestine, or the rights and political status enjoyed by Jews in any other country."*

This set out the British policy of favouring a homeland for the Jewish people in Palestine provided that nothing should prejudice the existing civil and religious rights of non-Jewish communities.

Unsurprisingly perhaps, this wasn't viewed favourably by the Palestinian Arabs who felt relegated to being "non-Jewish communities" and who saw no mention of any political rights. A few days later the full text of the Sykes-Picot Agreement was published in the Russian Bolshevik press and the Manchester Guardian. The difficulties the Balfour Declaration would cause through both its practical implementation and its inherent contradiction with the Sykes-Picot Agreement were very much underestimated.

Motivated by the fall-out from the Sykes-Picot Agreement and the Balfour Declaration, the British and French in an attempt to appease the Arabs and show they were committed to long-term self-determination in the region, now issued the Arabs with a declaration. The Anglo-French Declaration of 1918 committed them to emancipation and establishment of national governments – although the word "independence" was not used.

NEGOTIATIONS FOR THE PARIS PEACE AGREEMENT 1919:
Lloyd George saw the Middle East as a blank canvas on which to draw a new order. His idea was that Jewish demands for a homeland could be satisfied along with Greek territorial claims (they had been an ally for the last two years of the war) and also Armenian and Kurdish desires to carve out nations, at the same time as meeting the Hashemite's aspirations for self administration in the region. The French, under Clemenceau could see that because of the Balfour Declaration and Britain's extensive incursions into Lebanon and Syria under General Allenby they would not have the influence they had thought in 1916 when making the Sykes-Picot Agreement, although they still wanted control over what they called Greater Syria. The British weren't keen on France maintaining a strong influence in Syria and Lloyd George for his part was torn between a desire to rearrange the Middle East according to British plans, and keeping France as an ally. Many in the British government wanted to exclude the French from Syria completely but as much as Lloyd George wanted the French out of the Middle East, he didn't want to lose them as allies. Accordingly he made a "gentlemen's agreement" with the French leader Clemenceau in which the French were willing to give up their control over northern Iraq where Britain had oil interests and concede Britain full control over Palestine if they were left alone to govern Syria and Lebanon.

Clemenceau was willing to agree to this as he was keen that Britain agreed to certain of France's own demands against the Germans.

The Arabs, led by Feisal, thought Britain would look after their interests as promised by T.E. Lawrence during their uprising against the Turks. They counted on the renewal of the old Anglo-French rivalries and expected the British to support them against the French. In addition the Americans were only too ready to try and influence outcomes in favour of self-determination. Thus the parties entering the Paris talks had much to negotiate over and a fluid situation on the ground with conflicting ideals or aspirations amongst those around the table. The Zionists and Arabs were not party to the talks, but Feisal and Weizmann were each invited to present their cases; Feisal first having completed a tour around Syria and Palestine to gauge support for his plans – which he failed to achieve in the predominantly Christian and pro-French Lebanon. Despite this, the French were still unhappy that he had been invited and wanted him excluded completely. They did not want to annexe Syria to Arabia, as it was a separate country and they feared the Arabian influence of such a monolithic Arab nation.

Weizmann being keen to show the Americans and British that he had agreement of the Arabs to his plans submitted the Zionist's claim on Palestine on behalf of the Jews. Feisal on behalf of the Arabs was in harmony with this, and in 1919 the Feisal-Weizmann Agreement came into existence which promoted the close co-operation between the Arab state and Palestine within geographic boundaries to be defined after the conference, and which would allow large-scale Jewish immigration whilst protecting the rights of Arab farmers. Feisal's agreement was however dependent on Arab independence.

The difficulty of what to do with Syria, the question of what role the Arabs should take, also vexed the Americans who set up a Commission with a view to its reporting to the Conference. This took local soundings and found overwhelming anti-French sentiment. It proposed an American Mandate instead of a French one (never a real possibility) and pointed out that a "National Home" was not the same thing as a Jewish state but its findings were never to be presented before the treaty was signed.

Meanwhile in Turkey, following the signing of the Armistice in November 1918, the Italians decided to occupy parts of the Turkish mainland which they had been promised. Also, with British encouragement, the Greeks who had since their independence in 1831 entertained an ambition for a new Greek empire encompassing all lands that had once had Greek influence, invaded Anatolia. These actions encouraged the first stirrings of Turkish nationalism which were then emerging under the leadership of Mustafa Kemal.

THE TREATY OF VERSAILLES: In June 1919 the peace treaty was eventually signed by Britain France and Germany, and came into force in January 1920. A key element was the Covenant of the League of Nations. The treaty also dealt with amongst other things territorial concessions to be made by the Germans, including reparation payments to be made - which finally ceased only in 2011. It did however leave a number of things to be resolved, and the other Central Powers on the German side including Turkey were dealt with by way of a number of minor treaties, which included the Treaty of Sèvres signed in 1920 and the Treaty of Lausanne signed in 1923.

The League of Nations, formed at the end of the war, established a mandate system. A mandate was a legal status for certain territories transferred from the control of one country to another and containing the internationally agreed-upon terms for administering the territory on behalf of the League. A mandate was fundamentally different from a protectorate in that the Mandatory power undertook obligations to the League of Nations as well as to the inhabitants of the territory. Some said that creation of the three mandates of Syria, Palestine and Mesopotamia was simply a device created by the Great Powers to conceal their division of the spoils of war even though they were legal and administrative instruments and not geographical territories; the territorial jurisdiction of which being subject to change by treaty, capitulation, grant, usage, sufferance or other lawful means.

THE TREATY OF SÉVRES: Towards the end of 1919 Britain was starting to feel the financial strain of its continued occupation of Syria and began to retreat in the face of French demands. The French, determined to have their administration run Syria with virtual *carte blanche* to govern the country, were now the key power that the Arabs had to contend with. Other than the Sykes-Picot Agreement the French had made no promises to the Arabs during the conflict, but nonetheless did make concessions now, and allowed an independent parliament with the right to levy taxes and make laws provided the Arabs supported the French mandate. Feisal agreed, and this became known as the Feisal-Clemenceau Agreement. Feisal though did not have strong support, least of all from the growing nationalist movement and he was not helped by the resignation of Clemenceau soon after having made the agreement. Millerand, his successor as Prime Minister, was not interested in appeasing the Arabs so Feisal found himself with a basic choice of either to side with the French and sanction their crushing of the nationalists, or to abandon all dealings and go into opposition. He chose the latter and in 1920 the Feisal-Clemenceau Agreement was declared null and void and the nationalists (the Syrian National Congress) declared independence with Feisal as head of state. Palestine was declared part of this new kingdom and subsequently Feisal's brother Abdullah was proclaimed King of Mesopotamia. In Lebanon however, Christian groups now proclaimed their own independence from this new Syrian state. Understandably the British were concerned at the Syrian National Congress's claims in Palestine and Mesopotamia, particularly as the French at this time did not appear to have enough troops in the country to seriously oppose Feisal.

Meanwhile unrest was growing in Palestine following the declaration of independence by the Syrian National Congress, and violence erupted in Jerusalem between Arabs and Jews. At the conference at San Remo in Italy held by Britain, France, Japan and Italy to settle the Middle Eastern mandates there was much debate before the Balfour Declaration was ultimately accepted as agreed Allied policy. Concern was expressed on behalf of the Vatican that the Catholics in Palestine should be administered by the French however it was finally resolved on 25th April 1920 that Britain should have the mandate for Palestine - incorporating the Balfour Declaration, together with Mesopotamia (Iraq as it became after 1921) and France should have Syria. The French were adamant in their refusal to recognise Feisal as King of Syria; arguing that there was no reason that they should have a weaker mandate in Syria than Britain had in Palestine and it was at this point that the British became resigned to the French dealing with Syria how they pleased. It appeared that it was the Arabs who came off worse at this conference, with no recognition for their declared independence, and the intrusion of a Jewish national homeland in Palestine without any ability for the indigenous Arab population to assert their political rights.

The French now issued Feisal with an ultimatum to cease all attacks or they would occupy Damascus and depose him. They started to build up forces and by June were in a position to attack the Arabs. Poorly armed and not entirely united, Faisal's forces were routed. Now that Syria was entirely in French hands Feisal was exiled.

Meanwhile, amid much unrest between nationalists and supporters of the leaders of the old Ottoman regime, the Turks signed the peace treaty at Sèvres on 20th Aug 1920. This treaty proved to be unworkable; at least, it was not likely to lead to lasting peace for it contained some provisions which many considered outrageous. Greece was given territory right up to the suburbs of Istanbul together with the port of Izmir. Syria would gain much of the southern territory and the Kurds would receive autonomy. A greater independent Armenia was to receive access to the sea and large areas of what is now eastern Turkey. Almost immediately the Turkish Nationalists declared the signatories guilty of high treason and ethnic cleansing quickly followed, resulting in collapse of the Armenian army and territory being given back to the Turks. What remained was taken by the Russians and became the Armenian Soviet Socialist Republic. In 1921-22 Mustafa Kemal, leading the nationalist Turks, started to evict the Greeks from western Turkey in what became known as the Turkish War of Independence, whilst the British and French took no positive action to stop them. The process was effectively completed when the original Greek population was reduced from more than 2 million to some 150,000, the formally neutral Istanbul had been re-occupied and the Ottoman monarchy swept away. The Treaty of Lausanne (1923) now settled the future of Turkey and finally brought peace to the country for the first time since 1911. There were however two parties absent from the treaty; the Armenians and the Kurds. This was to cause further unrest in the Caucasus which continues to the present day.

HASHEMITE REVIVAL: The Treaty of Sèvres had been based more on the ambitions of the victorious allies rather than any real agreement on how to build peace in the Middle East. For whilst the old Ottoman influence was dead and four new countries had been created; Syria, Lebanon, Palestine and Iraq, their boundaries took scant account of the wishes of the inhabitants or the economics or geography of the region. The Zionists had perhaps gained most with Palestine being placed under a British mandate as they had sought, and Britain being obliged to implement the Balfour Declaration.

Following the award of the mandate to Britain the population of Mesopotamia (Iraq), being not too enamoured with having fought the

Turks only to gain a change of masters, commenced a full scale revolt against the British. This proved a costly drain on Britain's resources and Feisal had been gone barely a year from Syria when the British brought him back to power and installed him as King of Iraq.

At much the same time his brother Abdullah was installed as Emir of Trans-Jordan (the Mandate for Palestine permitted the British to make separate provision for the land to the east of the River Jordan) and so in May 1923 the Emirate of Trans-Jordan was recognised as a national state. The brothers' estranged father, Hussein, still had pretensions of being the ruler over a wider Arab nation but the British recognised him only as King of the Hejaz in the Arabian peninsula – where his power was not that strong being mostly bolstered by bribes of local tribes using subsidies from the British. Other parts of Arabia were ruled by Ibn Saud a key rival and adherent to the Wahhabi sect of Sunni Islam. The British sought Hussein's signature to the Treaty of Versailles, which he refused. This ultimately resulted in the ending of his subsidy and British support, thus weakened he was vulnerable to further attack from Ibn Saud, who in 1924 launched an offensive against the Hejaz and took Mecca. Hussein abdicated in favour of his son, Ali bin Hussein, who in turn abdicated in 1925 following various mutinies, and the Kingdom of Hejaz now ceased to exist. It was not until 1928 that Ibn Saud finally accepted the borders of Trans-Jordan with Abdullah.

IRAQ: The question of the Mosul oilfields in Kurdish Mesopotamia had not been resolved at Lausanne but had been referred to the League of Nations who in 1925 declared in favour of continued Iraqi control. In the same year an oil concession was granted providing a royalty income for the government. A new treaty was signed with the British in 1930 and in 1932 Iraq became the first of the countries under the Mandates to achieve independence. The dominance in Feisal's regime of the minority Sunni Arabs was to be an inherent weakness. In 1933 Feisal died, to be succeeded by his son Ghazi bin Feisal. A military coup in 1936 effectively swung power into the hands of a nationalist army. Ghazi's son Feisal II succeeded him as King of Iraq upon his death in an accident in 1939.

THE SITUATION IN PALESTINE: Back in Palestine violence had broken out between the Arab and Jewish populations. Representations were made to the British government by both sides; with the Arabs fearing that the increasing Jewish immigration would weaken their economic and political position, and the Jews unhappy at the diluting of the terms of the Balfour Declaration through the suspension of immigration (to appease the Arabs) and by announcements that Britain would not countenance a Jewish government over the non-Jewish majority.

The change in policy of the British government towards Turkey at the end of 1922, effectively allowing them to breach the terms of the Treaty of Sèvres, also signalled a change in policy back home in England. Lloyd George's coalition government fell apart under amongst other things heavy criticism of the way he had handled the Turks. He resigned and was replaced by a Conservative leader Bonar Law. The Zionists thus lost their most consistent ally. The future of Palestine now became more problematic under the mandate system as tensions grew between Arabs and Jews.

In 1922 the population of Palestine was estimated as: 589,000 Muslims, 83,000 Jews and 71,000 Christians. By 1925 the Jewish population had increased to more than 100,000. Things remained comparatively calm until 1929 when a series of attacks on Jews occurred which were put down to Arab concerns over Jewish immigration. These resulted in several hundred casualties on both sides and provoked the British to respond by restricting immigration and land purchase. Whichever way the British moved on this point they would offend either the Jews or the Arabs. In the end they reversed their decision and upset the Arabs once again.

With the rise of Adolf Hitler in Germany in the 1930s came a renewed exodus of Jews from Europe. The USA had imposed ethnic quotas in 1924 and so Palestine was the obvious choice of destination for them and its Jewish population further increased significantly. This influx provoked action from the Arabs, and the Arab revolt began – lasting from 1936 to 1939.

THE ARAB REVOLT: The British government's response to the revolt was to set up a commission of inquiry, its key recommendation was the partition of Palestine which would ultimately lead to independent Jewish and Arab states. Coupled to this would be limits set on immigration and a requirement to obtain Arab agreement if they were to be exceeded. This proposal was rejected by both the Zionists and the Palestinian Arabs; however it found favour in Trans-Jordan, Iraq and Saudi Arabia – which was its strategic intent – as the British were anxious not to alienate the larger Arab population on the eve of a world war where their support or acquiescence would be required. They had already concluded a treaty with Egypt to secure the Suez Canal as well as to provide key wartime facilities.

THE SECOND WORLD WAR: In 1939 Ghazi, the Iraqi ruler, died and was succeeded by his young son Feisal II. Anxious to secure their position in Iraq and in particular the oilfields, the British re-occupied the country in 1941 and then moved on to Syria to expel the Vichy French governor. The Zionists were now all the more anxious to secure a free immigration policy for Jews in Palestine in the light of the genocide happening in Europe, while in Palestine a number of Jewish freedom fighting groups emerged and carried out attacks on the British in Tel Aviv and Jerusalem. Turkey managed to remain neutral until February 1945 when it finally declared war on Germany. In the same year Trans-Jordan, Syria, Lebanon, Iraq, Egypt and Saudi Arabia formed the Arab League.

After the war France was in no fit state to reassert its authority over Syria and Lebanon and following elections in Syria, called by the Free French under General de Gaulle, and outbreaks of anti-French riots, they pulled out their forces in 1946. Similarly in Lebanon they had little choice but to withdraw leaving that country with independence and a population made up of equal numbers of Christians and Muslims, the latter being further subdivided into Sunnis, Shias and Druze.

The Emirate of Trans-Jordan was granted independence and now became the Hashemite Kingdom of Jordan in 1946 under Abdullah its King.

THE FORMATION OF ISRAEL: The Jews in Palestine began a revolt against the British Mandate in 1945. Little progress was made until the British Government decided to hand over the problem of Palestine to a special committee of the newly formed United Nations in 1947. This committee recommended that the Mandate be terminated and proposed partition into two separate Arab and Jewish states, with Jerusalem being dealt with separately. The Sinai Peninsula with its largely Bedouin population was to fall within the Jewish state. Although there were objections, not least from the Arabs and the British, the British Mandate did end and the State of Israel was proclaimed on 14th May 1948 with Weizmann becoming its first president. No corresponding Palestinian political entity had been created in anticipation of this and perhaps inevitably, the next day the countries of the Arab League declared war on Israel.

Israel won the war in February 1949 and emerged with territorial gains over land not included within the United Nations partition. These gains, including Jerusalem, but not the old city which remained in Arab hands, meant that Israel now comprised more than three quarters of the former Palestine Mandate area, with the remainder now essentially in two parts under the control of its neighbours. Clearly the Palestinians were the principal losers; they remained stateless and now physically divided. The area now known as the West Bank (including the old city of Jerusalem) was held by Abdullah and became annexed to Jordan while the coastal Gaza strip remained under Egyptian occupation.

ARAB-ISRAELI WARS: The 1950s saw an unsettled time within the newly formed Arab nations. The super-powers of the Cold War, the United States and the Soviet Union, were seeking to increase their influence. In Egypt in 1956, President Nasser decided to nationalise the Suez Canal, which resulted in Britain, France and Israel launching an attack and the closure of the canal for several months. Although militarily a success, this failed in its mission under pressure from the United States and the Soviet Union, with the allies being forced to withdraw. Concerns over the increasing influence of communists within Egypt and Syria led in part to those two countries forming a union in 1958 called the United Arab Republic which existed until 1961 under Nasser's leadership. This was hoped to be the start of a pan-Arab union, but it caused much disquiet in Jordan and Lebanon until ultimately Syria withdrew following a military coup. At much the same time Iraq became a republic following a coup in which the royal family was murdered. The end of the decade saw the emergence in Palestine of an Arab group known as Fatah, under the leadership of Yasser Arafat. Ten years later he was head of the Palestine Liberation Organisation (PLO) – more of an umbrella organisation for a number of groups.

In 1967 Syria and Egypt massed their forces against Israel, who in turn attacked and in the course of six days gained territory in Sinai from Egypt up to the Suez Canal, and roughly half of the Golan Heights from Syria. Jordan joined the fray and lost east Jerusalem and the West Bank for its trouble. Thus Israel now occupied extensively more than the area under the whole of the former Palestine Mandate. In 1973 in what became known as the Yom Kippur War, Syria and Egypt attacked Israeli forces in an attempt to win back their losses. The allies fared well initially but the Israeli forces very quickly drove them back and went on to make greater incursions into Egypt and Syria by the time a ceasefire was agreed less than a month after the initial attacks. Surprisingly this formed a basis for the start of peace talks which were initially orchestrated by the Americans, whose influence in the Middle East had long since eclipsed that of the British. A ceasefire line was settled through the Golan Heights and Israel retreated to the east bank of the Suez Canal.

By the early 1970s the Palestinians became more organised and in the guise of Fatah launched several attacks against Israelis in the West Bank. The PFLP (Popular Front for the Liberation of Palestine) famously hijacked a number of airliners in 1970 and blew them up in Jordan. King Hussein feared a West Bank ruled by the PLO, particularly as a large proportion of Jordan was made up of Palestinians, as this could lead to a threat to his authority. As PLO groups were using Jordan as a base for attacks against Israel he ordered his troops to attack these bases with the result that the PLO were expelled to Lebanon in 1971. Until this time Lebanon had been largely peaceful and was the most successful of the Arab states. However, internal tensions existed between the equally significant Christian and Muslim populations and with its sizable Palestinian refugee population it could not avoid being drawn into the Israeli-Palestinian dispute. Palestinian attacks on Israel from Lebanon drew reprisals which led to Christian-Palestinian fighting which in turn developed into Christian-Muslim conflict and full scale civil war which did not end until 1989.[†]

By the late 1970's though, the Israeli and Egyptian leaders were in peace talks facilitated by the Americans. These led to a formal signing of a peace treaty between them in 1979 following a summit between the Egyptian leader Sadat and the Israeli leader Begin at Camp David near Washington resulting in return of the Sinai to Egypt. Sadat had also tried unsuccessfully to settle the future of Gaza and the West Bank, but this remained at large.[‡]

[†] During this war there were periods when Lebanon was effectively at war with Israel, as in 1982 when the Israelis invaded southern Lebanon. By 1987 the main focus of Palestinian conflict had moved to Gaza and the West Bank where an uprising, the Intifada, presented a widespread challenge to Israel.

[‡] In 1993 the Israelis started talks with the PLO regarding Gaza and the West Bank in which the PLO agreed to recognise Israel's right to exist and itself gave up terrorism in exchange for an Israeli withdrawal from Gaza. 1994 saw a peace treaty being signed between Jordan and Israel and also the creation of a Palestinian Authority with Arafat its president. However, peace was not to come that easily for the Palestinians and relations with Israel deteriorated. Over subsequent years some of the more extreme Muslim groups, such as the Islamic Hamas, attacked Israel which led to various incursions into southern Lebanon and Gaza and the inevitable suffering of the Palestinian refugee populations in

THE PERIOD POST EGYPTIAN-ISRAELI PEACE TREATY: In 1979 Saddam Hussein came to power in Iraq. One of his first moves after removing internal opposition was to launch an attack on Iran. He saw the turmoil resulting from the replacement of the Shah with an Islamic Republic as an opportunity to make territorial gains in the Shatt al-Arab waterway separating their two countries. In the subsequent eight years he achieved virtually nothing and succeeded in bringing great debts to his country.[§]

THE LEGACY: It is hard to imagine what the Middle East would have looked like had some of the fundamental decisions taken in the first half of the last century been different. In particular, what might have been the effect had the British been less ambiguous with the Jews and the Arabs from the start; what if the Palestinians had had a strong advocate like Weizmann or been more organised at the time when the seeds were being sown for the new Jewish homeland in Palestine? A very different situation may have resulted, but what is certain is that the Middle East would still have become a complex tapestry of diverse peoples and religions with differing cultures and prejudices, and that this would still have resulted in a dynamic and exciting place in which to travel and live.

---

both areas. Hamas became the rulers within Gaza whilst the secular Fatah maintained dominance in West Bank, leading to a de facto splitting of the Palestinian Authority.

[§] In 1990 there followed an invasion and short-lived occupation of Kuwait which saw Egypt and Syria joining forces with America, Britain and France to liberate the Kuwaitis from the Iraqis.

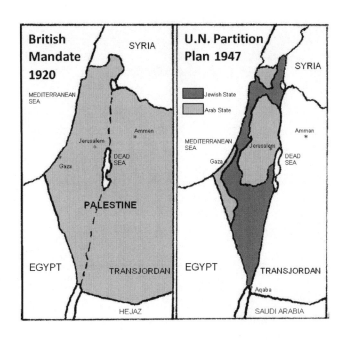

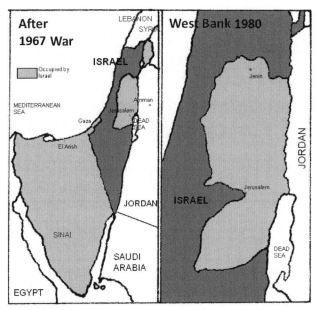

Partition of Palestine & creation of a Jewish State 1920 - 1980

5

FIRST STEPS IN AN ANTIQUE LAND

"Does the road wind uphill all the way?
Yes, to the very end.
Will the day's journey take the whole long day?
From morn to night, my friend."

Christina Rossetti - Uphill, 1861

The taxi from Aqaba took me at long last into the very centre of Amman; the Philadelphia of Roman times. By now it was dark and the city was illuminated by a few sodium lamps and what seemed hundreds of car headlights pointing in all directions as if their owners were driving madly around in a game of dodgems. There seemed no order to the traffic and the noise was deafening. We stopped outside a low terrace of what appeared to be concrete "lock-ups", having no regard for the queue of similar cars riding almost on our bumper and provoking a furious barrage of horn blowing and shouting. The driver, who had all the way from Aqaba kept a succession of smouldering cigarettes fixed between his lips now turned to me and indicated I was to get out. Clearly I was not at my destination, but this was apparently as far as the taxi was going. How far and in what direction lay Salt... I had no idea. I suddenly regretted that I had chosen as baggage a large metal trunk as well as a rucksack; my baggage allowance of one ton on board ship had earlier seemed such a positive advantage. I had even briefly pondered whether I might manage to include my motorcycle... thank goodness I hadn't. Suddenly I felt very isolated again; surrounded by scores of Arab men and boys all shouting incomprehensibly, seemingly at me.

I had received much advice before leaving England, although sadly none of it contained information on how to actually arrive at my Project in Salt. I remembered one thing, said to me by a neighbour in Suffolk who had travelled extensively as a Queen's Messenger; he'd advised that whenever he found himself at an unknown destination without an idea of where to turn next he would always pause, ignore his surroundings and light a cigarette. It was always important to appear confident and in control and not to appear like a fish out of water lest you be assumed to be a confused tourist ready to be taken advantage of. In the time it took to finish his smoke he would have identified his exit route and would then walk confidently and unhassled out of the airport. I decided that now was the time to try this tactic and started to roll up a *Gaulois*. This caused much interest and had the opposite effect to that intended. It seemed that only beggars and old men smoked hand-rolled cigarettes and that I was clearly in need of a decent smoke. A dozen arms were extended towards me each offering what I was later to discover was the ubiquitous Gold Star filter cigarette. Soon I had a glass of sweet mint tea in my hand, and apparently a dozen new friends! As soon as I thanked them, cries of "*Inglesi*" went up and all wanted to try out their English language skills. It transpired several spoke it well and soon I was loaded into another *servees-taxi*, with assurances that for a few *fils* it would take me up to Abdali Station the "bus station" from which onward transit to Salt could be made. A portly businessman type who was apparently travelling the same way volunteered to see me safely onto the next stage of the journey and explained in unexpectedly good English the *servees-taxi* system which operated like a bus service, charging a fixed rate for a fixed route and only departing with a full complement of five occupants – a very cheap if rather intimate way to travel in view of the average build of the local population I had encountered so far. Only as my trunk was loaded into the boot of the ancient Mercedes did I glance at the shop outside of which we had all been gathered for the last half hour – it sold Johnny Walker whiskey, now I felt I was in familiar territory.

There being nothing to see in the dark on the hour long drive up into the hills to the west of the capital the remainder of this journey seemed almost routine. Had it been daylight I would no doubt have been aware of the atrocious road conditions and the interesting driving techniques adopted by much of the Jordanian taxi driver population; namely their reliance on their apparent ability to see around blind corners and to create a force field around the car merely by use of sound waves emanating from the car's horn, but I was tired and despite the continual bumps in the road and incessant hooting spent most of the time dozing. This also had the advantage of avoiding the persistent questioning from the other occupants of this shared taxi which was beginning to lose its novelty. My first sight of the Holy Land Institute for the Deaf therefore came late in the evening and in the restricted street lighting gave no impression of the nature of the school or its setting on the side of hill in this ancient town. That day I had been on a ship, travelled in a motor launch and three taxis along endless miles of desert highway and was well and truly worn out, food and sleep was all I wanted but it was to be some hours still before I could call the day over.

The town of Salt with a population at that time of about 35,000 was a picturesque settlement nestling on the side of green hills to the west of the capital Amman on what used to be one of the main routes from Amman to Jerusalem. In the nineteenth century Salt's springs, of which there were three, formed an attractive focus for the settlement. One was for filling water bags and watering animals and the others were for ablutions; with men and women each having a separate spring. They were subsequently bridged over. The presence of a good water supply was no doubt an attraction for early settlers, as well as the more modern Arab Pharmaceutical Manufacturing company whose factory adjacent to the Institute employed more than 300 Saltis. Many of the population worked at the nearby cement factory in Fuheis, while others commuted to Amman or remained employed in agriculture upon the terraced former vineyards now cultivated with olives and fruit trees.

Nineteenth century Salt was described by Johan Burckhardt (1784 - 1817) the Swiss traveller who rediscovered Petra, as the only inhabited place in the province of Balqa. The population were apparently most independently minded (a euphemism for lawless) and resisted several attempts by the *pashas* of Damascus to subdue them. There were then 400 Muslim and 80 Christian families in the town and all lived "in perfect amity and equality". There was still a castle at that time where one of the three principal *sheikhs* resided. It was said to be well-built and surrounded by a wide ditch and from inside there was a subterranean passage in the limestone leading down to one of the main springs in the town which was used at times of siege. The population were mostly employed in agriculture in fields some 8 miles distant where wheat and barley was grown along with "vast quantities of grapes", the latter being dried and sold in Jerusalem.

The author and traveller Laurence Oliphant (1829 – 1888) later also described Salt; where the castle was now only in "tolerable repair" and where the houses were so tightly packed together and clustered one above another along the streams up to the hill crests such that one might possibly climb from the bottom to the top of the town by mounting each flat roof in turn. By this time the population had grown to 6,000 - twice the number in Burckhardt's day. This growth was attributed chiefly to the establishment in the town of the seat of government and Salt having become the centre of commerce for the whole region east of the River Jordan. Interestingly, his view of the local population differed from Burckhardt's in that he describes them as hitherto constantly quarrelling with each other or fighting with the Bedouin. Perhaps Burckhardt had acquired some rose-tinted spectacles in the course of his travels around Jordan and Petra.

In the 1920s the Emir (later to be King) Abdullah came to Salt which was then still a provincial city, but the largest in Trans-Jordan with a population of between 15,000 and 20,000 people. He founded various government departments and subsequently moved them to Amman. The city was an important market place for the Bedouins of Balqa and the citizens of Salt were still exporting some 5,000 to 7,000 tons of raisins to

Jerusalem and Jaffa (now Tel Aviv) annually. The grapes were also eaten and used to brew the alcoholic drink *arak*. By 1939 however the vines had all been wiped out by the plant lice *phylloxera*. The castle referred to by the early travel writers was destroyed by Ibrahim Pasha and I could find no signs of its remains.

This was the town which was to be my home for the next twelve months or so.

6

HOLY LAND INSTITUTE FOR THE DEAF

"At last he rose, and twitched his mantle blue:
To-morrow to fresh woods, and pastures new."

John Milton - Lycidas, 1638

The Institute, housed in what was originally one of the first medical facilities in Trans-Jordan, was located at the top of winding narrow steps leading up from the main town square. Entering through old iron gates from the road above I found myself deposited by the taxi outside an old limestone-faced structure which had comprised the main hospital building and which was now clearly in disrepair. There were some window openings blocked up with concrete and several suspicious cracks which appeared to go right through the structure (the result of shelling by the army I was later told). The hospital began its life as an Anglican mission complex in 1883 serviced by the Church Missionary Society under the auspice of the Anglican mission in Jerusalem. It became a hospital in about 1904 at a time when there were so few such facilities in the Ottoman governorate that it received patients from all over the Arab world. Upon the outbreak of the First World War the site was used by Turkish troops until after the Arab Revolt when in 1922 King Abdullah funded its expansion to meet the growing needs of Trans-Jordan. Another more modern hospital was subsequently built in Salt and the facility was virtually abandoned as medical centres were established in Amman, the new capital. The site then became an out-patient clinic but by 1933 had to be closed down due to financial difficulties. There continued some occupation of the site through the presence of an old people's home which at the time of my arrival occupied a small wing of the Institute housing no more than about a half a dozen elderly women.

The Holy Land Institute for the Deaf was founded in 1964 by Father Andeweg (Rev. Dr. Arie J. Andeweg 1932-1999) under the first Arab Bishop of the Diocese (Jerusalem) Najib Cubain. Andeweg, a Dutch Anglican clergyman, had earlier founded the Father Andeweg School for the Deaf in Loueizeh in Beirut in 1957 with the aim of; "providing oral education, rehabilitation and other services for deaf children of all cultures and religions without any discrimination; and to create a world where every deaf child was loved and protected and in which every child could develop to her/his full potential". Father Andeweg was a much honoured and inspirational force amongst the deaf community of Beirut and others who sought to help them. He grew up aware of the problems facing deaf people; his mother was an educator for the deaf and this may have in turn inspired him to make deaf education his life's vocation. After earning a degree in speech therapy he studied Theology at Oxford University and was ordained into the Anglican Church. Throughout his life he took courses in speech therapy and ran rehabilitation programmes for the deaf and mentally disabled. Later in life he acquired a doctorate in Special Education from the University of Minnesota. Not only could he speak Dutch, English, French, German and Arabic, but also he was widely respected for his fluency in sign language and ability to teach the partially deaf to communicate. I met him several times during the course of my stay in Salt and could vouch for the inspirational example which he set.

His Majesty King Hussein was invited to open the Institute in Salt in 1964. The school started modestly with thirty-two pupils and four teachers – numbers being restricted by the limitations of the accommodation. By 1967 some prefabricated buildings had been purchased and it became possible to expand the facilities. Father Andeweg continued to divide his time between Salt and Loueizeh until in 1977 Brother Andrew de Carpentier – another Dutchman - was invited by the Bishop to come from Beirut to be the new Director of the school. In 1978, the year before I arrived, Brother Andrew was joined by the Swiss family Grossenbacher who helped to establish a vocational training department. Seventy-five children now resided at the school and in all there were twenty-one staff including some local girls employed to undertake house-keeping and laundry work.

I knew none of this history as I made my way, seeking the Director Brother Andrew, into a large hall where voices could be heard above the sound of pots and pans being washed. Greeted by a heavily accented ginger-haired goatee-bearded man with a pronounced limp, who I learned was called Joshua (and whom I subsequently discovered to have only one leg), I was led to the table where sat at the head was a thin, heavily bearded and rather bald priest. There were others around the table, but my attention was drawn to the strangely attired man whose warm greeting beckoned me over and offered me food and tea. I was not expected of course – there had been no way to forewarn anyone of my arrival so there was a great deal of excitement. The room contained several long Formica-topped tables and was obviously the dining room for the school although there were no children present as they had not long been taken up to the boarding house. Shortly I was taken there too as Brother Andrew was anxious to introduce me before they had finally all been put to bed. Warning me that it would be noisy he and Joshua led me up a rough tarmac drive under a short avenue of pine trees to a long stone, arch-fronted boarding house. The arches were in-filled with green metal framed windows and the single storey building was brightly lit from inside. Loud shouts and lots of banging and scraping of chairs could be heard through the door, sounding rather as I imagined it would given that more than seventy children aged between four and fourteen were being marshalled reluctantly to bed; but I had no preconceived idea of what it would be like to become a part of this melee. Suddenly I was in the thick of it; the sound grew more intense and I felt more than a little overwhelmed. I watched as Brother Andrew gained the children's attention by a simple gesture of his hand and then proceeded to tell them who I was – at least I assumed that was what he was doing – his hand movements and facial contortions conveying meaning to his audience although to me it appeared he was performing some kind of complicated mime. Joshua supplied a translation for me and said "You need to say hello to the children". I think I was in shock as I had no idea what to do and must have stood for a full minute smiling inanely until suddenly a dozen hands were pulling at my sleeves and arms as each child wanted to draw my attention to themselves so that they could greet me personally. I felt a mixture of bewilderment at not understanding anything and panic at my complete isolation – what had I let myself in for? Only later did I appreciate the irony given that they were the deaf ones and I was the one who had all means of communication at his disposal. It had been a very long day and I had been running on adrenaline for most of it, so after a quick tour of the flat on the first floor of the old hospital building which I was to share with Brother Andrew I collapsed into my sleeping bag on a child's metal bed a foot shorter than me and was dead to the world without further thought or care.

Next morning I awoke to find myself disorientated until I remembered all that had happened on the previous day. Setting out to explore the place and meet the people who were to become my family for a year, it took only a few seconds to appraise my room (or cell) which comprised a concrete box little bigger than our garden shed at home, with a single window and an enormous stepped crack in the external wall through which I had a clear view of the pine trees which surrounded the building. I discovered a small pink gecko in this crack just above the window; it eyed me curiously but otherwise made no movement. The only furniture was a small metal bed with a foam mattress, clearly borrowed from the children's boarding house – I would have to do something about that urgently if my 6'3" form was to spend any length of time in this cot! Along one wall was a bank of shelves on which were neatly stacked classroom materials. Illumination was provided by a single bare bulb hanging from the ceiling which reflected light around the faded green hospital walls and chocolate brown flush door. I suddenly felt deflated; I'd been warned about culture shock, and wondered if this could be one of the signs. I really would have to see about making this storeroom into a more comfortable haven I thought, as I stuck one of the big posters I had brought with me from home over the gaping crack in the wall.

The accommodation through which my room was accessed comprised a small flat with two bedrooms, one being my host's and the other an empty guest room; a corridor with small kitchenette facilities; a large comfortable looking living space with arm chairs and rugs and a small bathroom with WC but no hot water completed the facilities. Leading out onto the first floor landing at the top of the stairs was another corridor with several rooms off, only two of which appeared to have a door or frame, the others were in varying states of disrepair. The first room with a door was the home of Aniseh the diminutive chain-smoking Lebanese housekeeper and her two adult nephews Niko and Elias, the second was their bathroom.

Downstairs one half of the building was sealed off and the remainder comprised more dilapidated rooms, some filled with barrels of paraffin or diesel, others with sacks of cement. At the rear were two large rooms which served as a laundry, leading out down concrete steps to a grassy area for hanging out washing. Two giggling maids seemed to be engaged in lighting a small paraffin stove under a huge cauldron of soapy water, this enterprise looked extremely dangerous to me and I backed out rather quickly to go and find the kitchen where breakfast had been promised. This large hall was distinguished from the other rooms by its hideously coloured two-tone orange walls and columns and fluorescent strip lights. This was the workplace of Badrieh the Egyptian cook; her addiction seemed to be for strong Arabic coffee….and the ubiquitous Gold Star cigarettes. I later discovered that Badrieh shared this room with a variety of wildlife, and not just the ever-present cat. Late one night I came down to steal some milk from the kitchen fridge having run out in the flat upstairs. Switching on the fluorescent lights I noticed with the first flash of the tubes that the floor was unusually dark. I gave this little thought until the second flash of the lights illuminated the room and I noticed that the darkness had now turned patchy. By the third flash I realised that the floor had been covered by thousands of cockroaches, but by the time the fluorescent tubes gave out their steady light these had nearly all disappeared. Where they went I had no idea, but I made a mental note never to visit at night again. I'm not sure that I wasn't more disturbed though by the rat which took up residence in the refrigerator, or rather in the enclosed area containing the compressor underneath the food box. Niko and I were asked to deal with this unwanted guest one day and having only large sticks to use as weapons we proceeded to upend the fridge so as to force the rodent to emerge into the open. We had already closed all windows and doors and blocked up the drains so there was nowhere for it to escape to and soon we had the rat running around the kitchen as we chased it yelling loudly and swinging our cudgels wildly. It was soon clear that the rat was likely to get the better of us being more nimble and very adept at avoiding being splatted against the floor, and as we rested to consider new tactics the main door was suddenly opened by one of the teachers who passing by had chosen to investigate the disturbance. Sensing an opportunity, the rat made a bee-line straight for the opening door only to be inadvertently stepped on and killed by the teacher as he crossed the threshold.

Due to the sloping nature of the land upon which the buildings had been constructed there was a lower ground floor underneath the rear of the kitchen which had its access directly from the compound. One wing comprised a small flat which was home to the Swiss family; Joshua and Dineke Grossenbacher and their two young sons Andy and Peter. I was to come to see this flat as a peaceful haven away from the often exhausting activities and demands of the deaf children; it combined relative comfort with a welcoming feel and most importantly it was the only place at the Institute which had been made to really feel like a home. Once a month I was invited as a guest in the evening to share some real meat such as a beef steak and a cool bottle of Amstel beer which had been generously provided with the support of the family's friends back in Switzerland.

To appreciate what a luxury this was it is necessary to describe a typical meal at the school. We all ate together with the children, so at mealtimes nearly ninety people would sit together in the dining hall. Rice would be the staple food occasionally substituted with spaghetti and on very special days, potatoes. On a day when meat was provided this would either appear in the form of slices of some form of processed tinned meat product misleadingly called *mortadella* (for it was not pork) or in the form of minced lamb. Given that only a couple of kilos would be used for the entire school it was a matter of great excitement to find more than a teaspoonful of meat on one's plate. The other key ingredient would be tomatoes which luckily along with rice, were in plentiful supply. There may have been other ingredients but I was never able to discern them. At that time I hated tomatoes, having spent many of my school holidays picking the wretched things. It wasn't long before I loved them, although it was many years later before I could again bring myself to eat spaghetti (for reasons I shall have to leave to the imagination). My favourite meal became *bamiyeh* stew which was made with "ladies fingers" and tomatoes which I would devour enthusiastically. A never ending supply of the locally-made flat bread or *khobis* would provide further bulk. Two children would run down to the bakers each morning and collect the day's supplies. At lunchtime a desert would be offered; usually fruit such as oranges, but sometimes rice pudding. We all seemed to thrive – even the dog, an Alsatian-cross called Bruno, who seemed to have become completely vegetarian. Breakfast and supper would generally comprise more bread (fresh in the morning but stale by the evening), olives, processed cheese slices, *humous* – made up from sacks of soya flour, purple onions and tea made with powdered milk or Arabic coffee. It is easy to see how the prospect of steak and chips *chez* Grossenbacher could become so appealing.

Food became a great preoccupation of mine and I grew to enjoy the particular green olives grown locally. That first winter they had become in short supply and one day it was decided that we needed to visit one of the nearby refugee camps to replenish our stores; stocks there were likely to be held back from the market and might be available for sale at a reasonable price. I volunteered to accompany the expedition and see what one of these camps was like and am glad that I did as I was able to sample the warm welcome of those who were forced to make the best out of what was obviously a bad situation. The densely packed concrete homes with their tin roofs looked barely habitable and the sewers were non-existent, many of the children were dressed in what I could only describe as dirty rags. It seemed impossible that their lot could be easily improved. We played our small part by paying them a good price for a boot-full of olives and returned to the school in sober mood.

Beneath the other wing of the main building there was installed a well equipped metal-workshop and store. This was Joshua's territory for he was a trained mechanic and was helping some of the older boys learn car mechanic skills as part of the vocational training programme at the Institute. I wandered around inside this Aladdin's cave of technology and precision – it was a Swiss workshop after all. Every hammer had its own special place and every tool had to be replaced exactly where it belonged and in the condition in which it had been found. Actually there was little technology apparent; a MIG welder, an angle grinder, a guillotine for cutting sheet metal and a Chinese manufactured bench drill seemed to be the most modern pieces of equipment, with the hammer and the welder being the most frequently used. Looking at the racks of angle iron hanging from the walls gave me an idea... I should be able to extend my bed by a foot. I had never used a welder but this was a good project with which to learn the necessary skills, and quickly too!

One of the hardest workers from amongst the local employees at the Institute was Abu Elias - as he was known, although his real name was Salim Fakhoury. He was almost a fixture at the school; he helped fetch and carry supplies for the kitchen and undertook much of the heavy construction and repair work despite his obvious great age. He had a deeply tanned face which was as gnarled as the trunks of many of the trees which were dotted around the school. In fact he told me that he had planted those trees from which I gathered he had worked on this site since the days when it had been a hospital. He had a cigarette constantly stuck to his bottom lip; one which he had rolled himself using some desiccated home-grown tobacco which stank appallingly even before it was lit and which he kept in a small engraved metal tin in the deep recess of the pocket in his grey woollen *qumbaz*. Abu Elias always wore this traditional dress with a wide leather belt whatever the weather, and I never saw him without his wrinkled features half covered by his black and white *kaffiyeh* worn in a style reminiscent of the Palestinian leader Yasser Arafat. He never set foot in Joshua's workshop; whether this was because he preferred to use his all-purpose mattock for just about every job from gardening to concrete mixing, or whether he had been caught using one of Joshua's precious tools like a mattock, I never knew.

Partly enclosed by a low concrete wall and partly by a few wire strands, the Institute's compound was not large, just under two acres I estimated. Running alongside a playground with metal swings and see-saw was a low stone-faced block of three small rooms with an even smaller concrete office building tagged onto the end. This was the classroom block. There was also one newer prefabricated metal building which housed two classes. This was where the deaf children received all their lessons, taught by five hearing teachers whom I encountered only at lunchtimes, for once their teaching duties were complete for the day they would disappear to their homes in various parts of the town and were never involved in after-school activities.

The education programme they followed was aimed at developing the children and to provide an all-round education to enable them to attain an integrated and meaningful role in society. An oral approach was adopted together with the principles of "Total Communication". Deaf and hearing impaired children would be accepted from the age of four into the nursery and into the kindergarten from the age of six. There followed seven years of elementary education culminating in two years of vocational training where the girls practiced sewing and academic subjects while the boys took on metal work and car servicing and repair.

The children lived in the boarding house, where I had met them on my first evening at the school. This was a single storey building of similar antiquity to the old hospital building which had probably originally been used as wards for the patients. It comprised a full length enclosed veranda at the front with some half-dozen square rooms leading off; all used as dormitories save for the central one which was a communal room with chairs and television. A small rear extension provided toilet and wash facilities, including an ancient paraffin water heater. Tagged on to the eastern end of the building was a very small apartment where the matron or housemother slept. At the time when I arrived the post had fallen vacant and night time duties were being performed by a deaf assistant named Lilly.

Now call me old fashioned but I like a bit of hot water in a bathroom, especially in the winter when there is only a single paraffin heater to warm a whole flat and outside temperatures are not dissimilar to those back in England, with low cloud and drizzle many days interspersed with heavy rain. One of my first tasks therefore became installation of an immersion water heater in my shared living quarters - I had no desire to trek up to the boarding house for a warm shower. A second-hand immersion heater had apparently been lying in the workshop for months gathering dust and it was a fairly simple job to plumb it in. Suddenly I was an "experienced" plumber and electrician and there was every chance I'd soon acquire the full set of building skills. That heater had to be fixed to the wall directly above the bath, every day I was reminded how secure I had made the fixings.

Despite the lack of most modern conveniences in my accommodation it did have a private telephone. This was an ancient device requiring the use of two hands to operate; one to hold the microphone stand in front of the mouth and the other to hold the earpiece to one's head. Brother Andrew sometimes used it - although the communication process was tortuous requiring first a call to the operator at the local Salt telephone exchange who would then call up the operator in Amman who would then call back when finally a line to Europe (usually Holland) had been obtained. This process could take more than a day! Given the archaic nature of the system I was surprised to learn that local calls within Salt were free and did not go through the operator. However, there was no telephone in the school office for official use and Brother Andrew felt that it would be useful to have this facility extended, although a separate line and number would be required. I was charged with making the necessary arrangements. Surprisingly this necessitated my climbing up the telephone pole in the street outside the office and untangling from the spaghetti like mess a "free" cable i.e. one which had a bare end and then running this into the building to be connected up with a telephone handset. Having first checked that it was live by the simple expedient of touching the two bare wires with my tongue... Well, they say we learn by experience and that was certainly a surprising experience, though thankfully not a lethal one. As we now had a working phone we could immediately make free use of the local telephone network the only hindrance being that we did not know our own phone number. The problem was happily solved some days later when the phone unexpectedly rang. The caller who had clearly dialled a wrong number obligingly repeated this to Brother Andrew and thus the office finally moved into the modern age. This was to be just one of many small improvements I was able to make during my time at the Institute.

By the time winter came along and the Jordanian weather started to behave rather more like the weather I was used to back home in England, I had become much more confident in my sign language and basic Arabic skills. My handyman skills having come on apace too and I found my days in the Institute busier than ever.

7

LIFE AS A VOLUNTEER

"I'm de'f in one year, en I can't hear out'n de udder."

Joel Chandler Harris - Uncle Remus His Songs and His Sayings, 1880

One of my key duties as the only volunteer working at the Institute was to assist in the boarding house in the evening after supper. This usually involved organising the watching of the television, a task I felt admirably qualified to take on. The children had no concept of sitting quietly while they viewed the interminable local news items; after all it didn't matter how much you shouted at the box if you were deaf. This was fine with me as my Arabic was not up to much, and as most foreign programmes were subtitled I learned very quickly how to watch television as a deaf person might. Everyone's favourite programme was "The Professionals" with the characters Bodie and Doyle racing around in an old Ford Capri. When this came on, which seemed to be several times a week, I would try and impose a degree of order amongst the audience, not because I wanted to listen particularly but because I wanted to read the incredibly bad subtitles which always seemed to accompany this series without having someone waving their arms in front of me. Having a dozen small arms pulling at my sleeve in order to attract my attention was a distraction I just had to ignore. Interestingly, they were invariably asking me "is this true" as the flash sports car side-swiped some criminal gang in a beaten up Jaguar, or someone got shot from an office block window. It was fairly easy to explain that this was not reality; in practice the Ford would never be able to make such a large dent in the Jaguar, and Bodie would never have hit that robber from that range with a hand gun... It became harder though to explain what was real and what was not in a drama documentary or a film... "Yes, that explosion did occur for real – but it was meant to, just for the camera"... "No, there were no people actually hurt there when it happened – they are just pretending – although it did really happen once...". I'm not sure that my sign language skills adequately explained the concepts I was trying to get across, particularly with the younger audience, whom I expected thought that in my home country of England there was as much violence as some of them had witnessed in theirs.

Not every night in the boarding house could I get away with a couple of hours just watching television, though I did try to sit down for some of the time as my days were incredibly busy and by about 7.30pm I was often more than ready for bed. Some evenings I would show cine film which I had managed to borrow from the British Council in Amman. The school had a 16mm projector and very soon I added "projectionist" to my long list of occupations. The choice of titles was very limited and most of those on offer seemed to be about natural history or oil exploration in the

North Sea, which was quite interesting and being in colour – there was no such thing as colour television – I had my audience captivated. The films were watched again and again. On one occasion I had forgotten to rewind the reel from a previous showing and only realised when I came back into the room half an hour later concerned at the silence and thinking the children must have all fallen asleep or run away. But, no, they were mesmerised by the backwards scenes unfolding on the screen (perhaps that should be folding...). Once, to my delight, I got hold of a copy of a scientific lecture on radioactivity made by my former headmaster A.F. Vyvyan-Robinson – I guess I was the only one who had a laugh at that one. Some evenings I would even stage a puppet show with toys that had been generously donated to the school. The stage was a bunk-bed moved away from the wall with a blanket draped down in front so that the puppets could perform on the top bunk and the puppeteer remain hidden from view. The hand puppets comprised an odd mix of soft toys and Disney characters. The plots were not memorable, being stories of my own devising, and often based on old television dramas and episodes of "The Professionals", but they were much enjoyed and constantly in demand.

On other evenings I might look forward to a quiet sit down in the flat with a selection of one of the many books donated to the school by departing "ex-pats" or simply a chat with Brother Andrew if he wasn't working late in the office – as he did most nights. I had devised a simple game from which I derived much amusement during my stay. It was all about idioms. My host had a great facility with languages (seven to be precise) but was nevertheless sometimes confused by certain foreign idiomatic sayings and expressions; for instance he once said to me "now the monkey's out of the sleeve" meaning to say that he could now see my true character – apparently in Dutch the expression is "*Nu komt de aap uit de mouw*". This gave me the idea to ask for a translation of other Dutch idioms and then to use them in English inappropriately, for example I might use the monkey phrase instead of "letting the cat out of the bag". After a while this proved such good sport that I thought I would have a go at playing the game in reverse; asking for the literal translation of an English idiom into Dutch and then lobbing it into a conversation at every suitable opportunity and hoping that it would be adopted – or at least subliminally embedded. Of course this required me to build up a supply of phrases and to try and make use of them on the evenings when we were both invited to the Swiss family's flat (for Dineke was also a Dutch speaker). My favourites were *kniehoge voor een sprinkhaan* (knee high to a grasshopper) and *dik als twee korte planken* (thick as two short planks). Scores were low, but results were always immensely satisfying.

With modern day communications it is hard to imagine that not so very long ago personal computers were unheard of, television was one or two channels of black and white grainy images and letters were the only realistic method of communication – and they could take weeks to arrive. I was far too busy fixing what needed fixing and carrying out all the duties of a general assistant to Brother Andrew in the office, Joshua in the workshop and Huda in the boarding house, to bother with communications and it was nearly six weeks before I realised I had not set foot outside of the confines of the school. The daily routine started with an early communal breakfast with the children and a short play in the yard before the teachers arrived to take up their duties. Next, I would report to either Joshua or Brother Andrew depending on what was scheduled for that day. Often there was a little office work to do such as typing correspondence with an ancient typewriter, but more usually there was something which needed mending or making involving plumbing, electrical wiring, digging drains, mixing concrete, carpentry, welding or painting. The list was long and I was able to extend it. I could see many things which could be done which would improve the quality of life but which only needed a pair of hands and enthusiasm to see them accomplished. Everyone was working to the point of exhaustion and had little time to spare to see to all that needed attention and certainly no time for any luxury.

Having moved on a little from novice status with my welding skills (already practiced on my bed) I was increasing in confidence and ability every day. It wasn't going to last of course. One bright day whilst welding outside the workshop I failed to protect my eyes properly and suffered the most excruciating soreness and indeed blindness for a couple of days. It was a good lesson to have learned and certainly taught me a healthy respect for my tools – to which I had access in abundance. I only wish I had also learned about cement burns, but that was to await another day. Not every day involved the same challenges. My very first job on my very first day in the school was to unblock the soil pipes leading from the children's toilets. A crowd of small children showed an unnaturally keen interest in my progress as I dug down to find and break open the sewage pipe where I judged the blockage to be. Then it dawned on me; they wanted their ball back.

Christmas and new year was inevitably a busy time. It started early – on 19th November, with the Muslim new year; in fact the first day of the new millennium (1400). Although the Institute was run as a Christian concern this was still a day to celebrate. Then on 5th December came St Nicholas's Eve, celebrated by the Dutch contingent (Brother Andrew & Dineke) when Dineke cooked her family a special meal to which Brother Andrew & I were invited. There was even a celebratory bottle of Amstel beer bought furtively from the ironmongers down in the town. The next day saw St Nicholas's Day celebrated by the family, to which again I was invited. By the time 25th December came around I was suffering a little from festival fatigue. The most important date in the school's calendar however was Christmas day. This was when all the children would receive a present purchased through the kind donations of those overseas supporters of the Institute. I was to go with Brother Andrew to Amman to buy some suitable gifts. Taking the huge Chevrolet Suburban, a former ambulance donated by the Sisters of Charity we set off one evening to the only toy shop in Amman. The store owner was very keen to sell us his latest imports and we duly loaded up with a good stock of drawing sets and bats and balls. Just as we were leaving the owner asked if the children might be interested in some old toys which were at the back of the shop. This was very old stock and apparently there was no demand for it and it could be ours for a modest sum! My jaw dropped when I saw what was stacked on the shelves; old Meccano sets, clockwork trains and cars and all manner of toys which would have been collectible back home. Many were wind-up including some marked "Made in US zone – Germany". We bought the lot and loaded them into the back of the Chevrolet. The plan was to take them back to Switzerland for either sale or display in a toy museum. Like two big kids we drove back to Salt eager to inspect our purchases more carefully.

That evening found us both sitting cross-legged on the tiled floor of the flat, a celebratory drink in hand from a partially empty bottle of Drambuie someone had considerately donated, taking it in turns to wind up the trains running round on our very own railway layout. Christmas day itself was a bit of an anticlimax after this. There was a party in the kitchen with all of the children receiving their presents from an honoured guest in the person of John another English volunteer who had travelled in from his Project at the Schneller School and obligingly dressed up in a Santa Claus outfit. Later that winter when it snowed heavily for the first time in many years, even snowing in Bethlehem, there was enough of the soft white stuff to build a sizeable snowman in the playground. We even climbed onto the low roof of the school office and took turns with the children to launch ourselves off into the drifts below. It was cold, very cold, and in my careful packing I had given no thought whatsoever to bringing a coat.

It transpired that Jordan was to have exceptional weather over the winter of 1979. Following a prolonged period of drought rain fell on the 2nd November in such quantity that there were flash floods in Amman and two children were swept away and drowned in the low-lying centre of the city while hundreds of houses were flooded or left surrounded by water with the occupants needing rescuing by civil defence volunteers. Cars were carried along like flotsam. A newspaper story under the headline *"Record rains cause havoc, deaths in Amman"* reminds me, a little surreally perhaps, that:

> *"...they saw what at first appeared a third victim lying limp across a railroad track; but it turned out to be a 14-year old girl who was waiting for a train so she could commit suicide. Apparently the girl was unhappy as the wife of a much older man who has seven children."**

Salt received more than ten times its average rainfall for that time of year and in early March a foot of snow!

This was exceptional weather of course, and as a rule water was a scarce resource carefully guarded. For this reason the mains water supply in Salt was sporadic, being turned on only once a week in the summer and perhaps twice a week in the winter. Consequently all homes had large galvanised iron water tanks on their roofs which the occupants filled from the mains. The school had a number of these water tanks on the classroom roof which each contained some 450 gallons but they did not provide sufficient capacity to last the week and I had the job of installing a further tank to ensure that the school toilets could continue to operate adequately in the summer. With a ready supply of willing young helpers the task didn't look like it would present too much of a challenge. I had simply to loop a rope around the new tank and drag it up a sloping metal ladder onto the flat classroom roof where it could be lifted onto concrete blocks. I duly briefed my enthusiastic helpers in my rather crude sign language; the strongest would be with me on the roof hauling on the rope and the remainder would be equipped with wooden poles and would stand below poking the tank to ensure that as it ascended it did not slide sideways off

---

* Jordan Times, 5th November, 1979

the ladder, for the ladder was but a foot wide and the tank more than three. All was going well until we took up the slack and had the tank straining on the rope, at which point I realised that I needed an extra pair of hands with me on the roof to grab a hold of the tank as it appeared above the low parapet and so stop it tipping backwards and falling out of its rope sling, which it inevitably would do if we didn't take correcting action. My first thought was to signal to the children below to get out of the way – shouting would be no good given their deafness, but I realised that without my taking the weight the tank would drop like a stone and crush those below. In a panic, I eased off my pressure on the rope enough to stop the tank ascending any further and frantically tried to sign with just my facial expression that the children should get out of the way and let us lower the tank back down. Eventually, without my contribution to the effort, the boys beside me weakened and the tank did slowly slide back down. What a relief. I had to sit down I was shaking so much. After several shots of strong sweet Arabic coffee I returned to a state of equilibrium and learning from the experience I adopted an improved technique and finally succeeded in the task. Henceforth I was always wary when Joshua asked me to undertake any task which involved plumbing. That is until one day when I was asked to install a water meter.

Surprisingly the school water supply was not metered at this time and it was decided that there would be a benefit to be had if it were. The work would simply involve my digging a hole near to where the supply pipe entered the property and disconnecting the tap at the first junction and then fitting the meter upstream of it. Given that the weekly supply of mains-pressure water wasn't due for a day or so this seemed a straightforward task; and so it would have been had not the town pumps been turned on a day early just as I was in the middle of fitting the connection. Again my panic was not detected by the small group of child spectators I had inevitably acquired. Instead I was the subject of great amusement and entertainment as an enormous water fountain was forced out of the unmade connection soaking me and creating a major flood. It was like trying to fix a leak in a submarine! It took the combined strength of Joshua and me to finally install the meter. The only consolation was that there would be no charge for the wastage, which must have been hundreds of gallons.

One of the highlights for the children every week was a trip to the local sweet shop to spend the few *fils* each child was allowed in pocket money. Whilst this event was greatly looked forward to it proved to be a very stressful outing involving escorting nearly the whole school down the road and trying to create some semblance of order as they jostled with each other trying to be first in line. The process was all very inefficient and not without risk, especially from passing traffic as no-one could hear the cars and so jump out of the way. The simple solution seemed to be to have the shop come to the school. This would both improve safety and enable me to buy the sweets in bulk down in the town and get the children better value for their meagre coins. The storeroom next to the office lent itself ideally to this operation and with minimal alteration to the door a counter was attached. First the pocket money would be distributed and then the shop was open for business. The older boys were still allowed to visit the local store and would delight in coming back and telling me how much cheaper it was in my kiosk. We soon stocked other small items like balloons and small toys but I made a point of still buying some of my stock from the local shopkeeper down the road, as I felt sure that income from the children must have provided a significant part of his little business.

I was always on the look-out for other things which would interest the children and which could occupy them in the afternoons and at weekends when school was over. As the weather improved I started to take some of the older children on walks around Salt. Opportunities were somewhat limited as this was dependent of having someone else to stay at the school to look after the remaining children. Sometimes Lilly would be available and Niko was always keen to start a football game, but generally I had to be on site so needed to find some other activity. I struck on the idea of pets. The Institute already had a cat and a pet dog called Bruno, a large black animal resembling an Alsatian crossed with a Labrador. Neither provided much entertainment as the cat only appeared at mealtimes and Bruno was primarily kept as a guard dog. What we needed were rabbits. These would also have the advantage of providing a few meals which would be a welcome addition to our limited protein diet. After a few days and with the help of several of the children I had two cages ready. These were constructed from a half of an old iron water tank and would provide luxurious accommodation for the new arrivals once I had worked out how to acquire them. In the end it was Abu Elias who procured two fine animals for me (*arnab* in Arabic).

The rabbits seemed content to be fed mainly on cracked wheat, but the children were keen to collect anything green growing within the confines of the school and feed this to them through the chicken-wired cage doors.

This supply was soon exhausted as the weather grew steadily warmer and I had to resort to procuring carrots from the vegetable shop down in the centre of Salt. One thing which seemed to grow in inverse ratio to the vegetation was the rabbit population itself. It seemed that they were taking advantage of the temporary "association time" granted them by the children while the cages were being cleaned out, and whilst I had been planning to increase the stock I could not keep up with the necessary cage construction. Already I had bisected the original cages and could not go on doing that. The answer of course was to start eating the beasts. I was surprised at how little resistance there was from the children who I thought might have become attached to the fluffy creatures; perhaps they were as hungry as I was. There was one problem – not everyone could eat them unless we could show that they had been dispatched in the *halal* manner. I brought Abu Elias along to perform this act, not that I was squeamish, but I felt that with his years of experience he would be better able to do this. It was a messy job and the poor animals seemed to take an inordinate amount of time to bleed to death. I was however quite taken by his novel method of skinning the carcasses which involved inflating them using the air from the workshop compressor – apparently this worked well with sheep, but it was somewhat of an over-kill with our rabbits. Still, the children enjoyed improvising glove puppets made out of the scalps and ears....

This wasn't the first time I had seen an animal killed in accordance with the requirements of the Muslim religion. One lunchtime when the whole school was assembled in the dining room there burst in a very excited man who rushed up to the stoves where Badrieh was standing, shouting at her such that I thought he might be about to attack someone. My suspicions were nearly confirmed when he grabbed a huge knife and still shouting ran back out of the building. Cautiously I followed to find out what was up, suspecting he was about to commit a murder in the street. I wasn't far wrong; apparently the taxi, of which he was the driver, had run into a sheep which lay badly injured by the roadside and he wanted to ensure it was killed in the correct manner before it expired of its own accord. He would have to pay the owner for his loss and the price would be considerable higher if the sheep could not be eaten.

At about this time the Institute's animal population was swelled by the addition of a hamster - who it transpired was a war refugee. He arrived one day in the back of the Chevrolet having been driven by Brother Andrew from Beirut through Syria. It seemed the building against which his cage had been constructed had been damaged or destroyed by shell-fire and he was the only survivor. He was not the first hamster to have been rescued and to have travelled across Syria, for like all pet Syrian hamsters he was a descendent of a litter found in Aleppo in 1930. Although hamsters had been first discovered by G. R. Waterhouse in 1839, none had been seen again until the zoologist Israel Aharoni came along. He came across a mother and her litter and managed to breed from four of the pups. The cage I had constructed for my hamster was a part of an iron water tank, with bars welded together from concrete reinforcement iron. The whole thing weighed as much as one of the children and was neatly finished in silver and yellow paint. This was my mistake. I had forgotten about the habit of hamsters to gnaw at their bars. Soon the silver paint had been removed exposing the red lead oxide I had used to prime the metal and the poor hamster's demise was assured. I fared little better with pigeons. Having acquired a pair which happily started to breed, quite quickly I found that the temptation of the youths in the neighbourhood to shoot them for food was too great and the pigeon population also went into rapid decline. Clearly my attempts at establishing a menagerie to amuse the children had only limited success.

Sometimes the continuous pressure of working so intensely in such a small community became a little over-bearing and I looked for any opportunity to escape for a few hours. For this reason whenever there was an excuse to drive one of the school's vehicles I was always keen to offer my services. For one thing, it was often a chance to see something different of the country, for another - I really enjoyed the experience. There were often jobs which involved driving as often items for the car repair workshop required collection from Amman or some other shopping might be needed. On special days there might be an expedition with the children when more than one vehicle would be taken; whatever the occasion I tried to make myself available – particularly if it coincided with my rest day. There was one difficulty however; my International Driving Permit obtained in England had an endorsement in very small print that it was valid everywhere in the world except one Central American country and for vehicles in Jordan with white number plates. I'd thought nothing of it at the time but it transpired that all private cars in Jordan had white number plates. In fact there were a multitude of colours: red for military and government vehicles, blue for United Nations, green for taxis and commercial, yellow for non-tax paid, but by far the most common was white – and that was the colour proudly displayed by the Institute's

Chevrolet. The Swiss family however, retained their Swiss licence plates and this was my opportunity. After a while and as my confidence grew i.e. not ever having had to show my licence, I noticed that the driving licence issued by the Jordanian authorities bore a remarkable resemblance to the old identity card I had been given when I worked temporarily as a stores porter in an Ipswich hospital and which for some reason I no longer recall I had brought with me. It was just the same, save for instead of having Arabic script it declared in plain English my name, function and date of appointment next to a creditable photographic likeness. I carried this with me everywhere thinking I could explain if asked that this was an English translation of the local licence. Its effectiveness was never tested as it was always my passport that I was asked to show if stopped. Later I found out that all that was required to obtain a driving licence was the ability to get in a car, start up, move off, stop, get out and hand over the fee. I realised that my card was probably a truer indication of my driving skills – at least it indicated that I could drive an articulated electric hospital cart along busy corridors.

Those skills were tested on several occasions, but the most hair-raising event was a short trip I made one time up the steeply winding hill behind the school. I was carrying half a dozen children at the time in a borrowed Peugeot estate car on a wet November day. I was well used to having the steering wheel on the wrong side by this time, but this particular car had a column gear-shift which was unfamiliar to me. At a particularly sharp and narrow hair-pin bend I encountered a lorry coming down towards me which gave no indication of giving way; its driver presumably seeing that there was sufficient room behind me to let him pass in the apex of the last turn. I fumbled with the gears to find reverse and get out of his way, when suddenly the gear lever came off in my hand forcing me to coast backwards all the way down the hill with the engine still in gear and with my foot on the clutch. I coasted around a series of tight bends as I tried to peer around the mass of excited children on the two rows of back seats through a misted window, all the time hoping there would be nothing coming up behind me. The drop at the side of the road was perilous and I was relieved when I was finally able to manoeuvre such that I could resume my journey in a forwards direction. I remember thinking that there was nothing quite like this on my driving test! (I'd been a motorcyclist for several years, but had only passed my car test just before leaving England.)

I always looked forward to working with Joshua as nearly every job provided the opportunity to learn or practice a new skill. Sometimes it was metal working, sometimes it was plumbing or building; Joshua either had the tool for it or the skill to make one if needed. He had been putting a lot of effort into building up his vocational training classes and made great use of the amply equipped workshop which was stocked with much of his own equipment and tools as well as those generously donated by friends from Switzerland. He had in the past been employed in repairing motor vehicles and it was this skill which if the older boys could be adequately trained would help them make a living for themselves and their families when they left the Institute. For this reason there were often cars waiting around the workshop in need of some repair. Having spent rather too much time lying on his back on the gravel surface under these vehicles Joshua one day decided that an inspection pit would be a most useful addition to the workshop facilities. The limestone rock which had for so long supported the structure of the buildings was to be a hindrance to his plan, but ever ingenious he decided to make use of the steeply sloping driveway at the side of the building to construct a block and cement double ramp onto which the cars could be driven, thus allowing full height standing room (for Joshua!) under the centre of the vehicles. The older boys helped in its construction using many stone blocks collected from the recently demolished mortuary nearby and all agreed that this facility would be a great asset. The structure was rudimentary and would not have been passed by any health and safety inspector in this country being simply two walls forming what was effectively a ski-jump – having no safety barriers whatsoever.

The day eventually arrived when I came to use the ramp to assist in the servicing of a large Chevrolet ambulance loaned to the school by Mother Teresa's Sisters of Charity. This particular vehicle was of the type with the engine in the cab beside the driver meaning that the driving position was far forward and on top of the front wheels (like that in a Volkswagen camper van). As I slowly approached down the slope and started to line up the wheels with the ramp I discovered the reason that the Chevrolet was in for a service... the brakes did not work! I was already committed to the ramp and rather hoped that the sudden change in incline of the slope to the level surface of the ramp would be sufficient to slow me down; if not, then I was about to experience the ski-jumping capabilities of a two-ton Chevrolet – somewhat akin to those of Eddie "The Eagle" (Britain's later ski jump competitor in the 1988 Winter Olympics in

Canada). Had I enough time to recall the principles of physics I would have realised that my best strategy would probably have been to open the door and jump out.... but I knew that a crash would then be inevitable as there were other cars parked nearby, including Joshua's lovingly maintained Peugeot. Instead I gripped the enormous steering wheel and with the foot brake flat on the floor I hit the front of the ramp with great precision and shot along at what seemed a reckless speed. Sitting at the front of a very long vehicle I had an unobstructed view of the sky... until the moment when the front wheels ran off the ramp! It wasn't quite the same as in that famous scene in the classic film "The Italian Job" when Michael Caine and his accomplices become perched over a cliff edge in a see-sawing bus; for one thing it was the front of the vehicle which had gone over, and for another, there was definitely no see-sawing as the ambulance had ended up nose-down firmly wedged over the end of the ramp. The poor vehicle was eventually recovered with the help of a jack and some heavy beams. I was never sure whether Joshua was cross that I'd nearly killed myself, or pleased that I'd had the consideration to avoid his beloved Peugeot.

There were to be numerous tasks and projects assigned to me during my year at the school but one of which I was most proud was the construction of a new classroom. The work was to be undertaken during the summer holiday when all the children had gone back to their homes and was to be completed before their return to school in September. An additional classroom meant that some of the children could stay on at school for another year which meant a great deal for their chances of getting on in life. The design was to be simple: concrete blocks with a corrugated sheet roof, a single door and small window. The foundations didn't need to be deep as the site chosen next to one of the other classrooms had bed rock just a few inches below the soil. What made this project memorable was the amount of concrete and mortar I was to mix by hand in the searing August heat. The cement mix quickly dried out and it was necessary to construct the block work as quickly as possible or it would be wasted. I was working single-handed and so had to keep going until all the mortar was used up. I don't think I have ever to this day undertaken such back-breaking labour. The building when finished was to remain in use for a number of years. The classroom would have won no design awards, but I felt that I was leaving a lasting legacy for the children.

Monday was my day of rest when I might undertake some small project for my own benefit such as making some furniture for my room or a hamster cage, or just as often I would have a lie in bed and then write letters and listen to one of the few cassettes I had brought with me. I had made an arrangement with the Amman office of British Airways whereby they supplied me with the occasional free copy of an English newspaper, usually the Times airmail edition, and when one arrived I would be absorbed for hours. Letters to and from home often took weeks to make the round trip (if at all) – the source of some amusement at the expense of my mother when I returned home. I had brought with me only six rolls of film to last a year and so was very frugal in selecting my photographic subjects but also meticulous in recording each shot. Whenever I had the opportunity I would hand the exposed film canister to a visitor who was returning to Europe and ask them to post it for me to the film processing company as I didn't want it to become lost in the Jordanian postal system. I would then send the index for each film to my mother who would shortly receive from the company the developed pictures (slides as it happens) and by this way keep informed of my activities. Unfortunately one of the first films I sent was lost and thereafter she had been unknowingly out of sequence with the chronology for months. I think she must have thought I'd gone mad as she told me my descriptions had made only partial sense to her. What amused me though was the word "partial"!

I enjoyed my days working in the office, particularly when in the winter it was wet and cold outside, as it contained one of only four paraffin heaters in the entire school. The benefits this produced were marginal though as the corrugated tin sheet roof offered zero insulation and the door, which opened directly onto the playground, was continually left open whenever there was a female visitor to the see the director. It was made very clear to me that no male should ever be alone in a room with the door closed if he was in the company of a woman or girl no matter what her age or marital status. This rule applied equally to the Arab teachers and to any western women who might visit. The concern was two-fold, firstly there was the honour of the woman or girl and secondly the reputation of the school to be upheld. On one occasion we received a visit from a female member of the British aristocracy and I was alone in the office at the time so made a point of propping the door open and explaining that this was for the benefit of both our reputations and the school's while we waited for the director to arrive. Only much later did I realise that this well-spoken visitor was the daughter of a baronet who had been a Maid of Honour for Queen Elizabeth at her coronation and must have been much amused at the suggestion that anything "improper" might be imputed by the local Arabs.

There was one occasion though when a most embarrassing incident with potentially serious consequences was only just avoided. It was my morning off and I was lying in bed dozing and savouring not having to get up at any particular time when one of the young maids came into my bedroom and started to mop the floor. She must have assumed that I was at work and luckily had not looked at the dishevelled bed in the corner of the room or else she might have noticed me lying half naked covered by only a crumpled sheet. I realised that in a moment she would turn and if she saw me awake, there could not fail to be an embarrassing situation. Quickly I grabbed my sheet and rolled noisily over to face the wall letting out what I hoped would pass for a loud snore, hoping that she would be startled but realising I was asleep would quickly vacate the room. This had the desired effect and she had the common sense to leave the cleaning of the rest of the flat until she knew I had emerged for lunch. Just as well, as I didn't fancy a visit from her father demanding that I marry the poor girl in order to preserve her reputation!

One rest day I decided to forego a lazy lie in bed in favour of going see a movie, and as the Rainbow Cinema in Amman was the only venue for such entertainment I thought it might be fun to hitch-hike into town and see a matinee performance. I assumed that any film would have been made in English and although inevitably subtitled into Arabic, would still be intelligible to me. This turned out to be not quite the case, for I was correct on the first point; "Lion of the Desert" with Anthony Quinn and Oliver Reed was indeed made in English but it had been *dubbed* into Arabic and had Italian subtitles. Clearly I was going to have to try and lip-read to make any sense of it, for although the actors waved their arms around a lot they certainly weren't using any form of sign language recognisable to me. It turned out to be an historical action movie, made in Libya and funded by Colonel Gaddafi, about patriots in Libya fighting in 1929 against Italian colonisation. There was much blowing up of tanks and not too much dialogue and so I settled back in my plush armchair to enjoy the performance in the packed auditorium. Soon the entirely male audience was getting carried away with the brutal action (which seemed to me to be particularly one-sided) for every time an Italian soldier was shot or injured or an Italian tank blown up (every five minutes or so) the whole cinema cheered and clapped. By way of stark contrast, on the rare occasions that an Arab was killed there was a deathly hush. Quite amusing at first, but this became rather unsettling when I realised that I must have been the only white European in a room full of Arabs baying for Italian blood! I left early – under cover of the darkness before the lights came up – just as a precaution.

Wherever I went the Jordanians I encountered were almost without exception most welcoming and hospitable. I understood that this was part of the Islamic culture - for Muslims were required to offer charity to the needy as one of the five pillars of Islam, but this hospitality was received from Christians and Muslims alike. It often went further than just looking after the needy; travellers were included in this category, which probably explained why it was so easy to hitch-hike around the country. I was to sample this hospitality one memorable day in Salt when invited with Brother Andrew to the home of one of the Christian members of the domestic staff at the Institute. I knew that we had a long-standing invitation to visit, but that we were hesitant to accept as the family was particularly poor and we did not want to impose a burden upon them. Inevitably we had to accept the invitation in order to avoid a sleight on the family and so one wet winter's day we weaved our way on foot through the narrow streets and up many winding steps until we arrived at the small stone-faced block which was the family's one room dwelling. We were sat down with cushions upon many coloured rugs and offered traditional Bedouin coffee while we were introduced to the family by the father of the household, a burly figure of some fifty years old and his wife whom I was told was several years younger. The eldest sons and daughters entered first followed by the remainder in descending order of age. Some of the older children were accompanied by their husbands or wives and themselves had small children. The room began to fill a little uncomfortably. I asked the girl who had invited us how many siblings she had and was amazed when she quoted a number in the high "teens", her mother she said, had had twenty one pregnancies! I naively asked whether they all lived here and was staggered to learn that they did as she pointed at a pile of mattresses in an alcove partially hidden by curtains. At night these were laid out on the rugs and the entire family slept in this one room which served as living space and kitchen as well. I couldn't rid my mind of the thought of how they managed to cope with living this way. This was more cramped than some of the homes I had seen in the refugee camp.

The meal which had been prepared outside on the steps was *mansaf*, a traditional Jordanian and Palestinian dish made of lamb cooked in a sauce of fermented dried yoghurt called *jameed* on a huge bed of rice and topped with pine nuts. It was placed on the floor in the middle of the room on a platter which must have been nearly three feet wide. As was the tradition, the father of the house selected some choice chunks of meat and handed these to his guests (with his right hand of course) before everyone helped themselves by making small balls of rice and sauce and popping them into their mouths. The soured yoghurt sauce and subtle spices made what was most definitely the finest and most memorable meal I had eaten all year. It would have cost the family significantly to provide this feast and we were certainly made to feel like royalty. It was some hours before we finished our coffee drinking and were able to make a respectable exit.

The opportunity to speak Arabic was everywhere around me both in school with the teachers and outside with the local shopkeepers and tradesmen, but whilst I had every chance to practice the little I had learned, the necessity was not there as sign language was what I needed for everyday communication in the Institute. Nevertheless I decided to accept an offer of lessons with Huda who was the best educated of the staff and whose language was traditional Jordanian rather than the Lebanese or Egyptian of some of the others. Learning the alphabet was fun as it then became quite easy to distinguish the twenty-eight main characters and so read the road-signs. We spent hours in the evening after the children were in bed running through basic greetings and requests which proved invaluable to me on my travels. It became easy to establish a rapport with drivers when one used classical Arabic greetings or responded with a grammatically correct reply. The delightful formal phrase *"Alla ysabbhak bilkhair"* - "God give thee a happy morning" was probably the most often used expression. At first when listening to the language spoken it was impossible to discern the end of one word and the start of the next let alone distinguish between the various unfamiliar vowel and consonant sounds but gradually my ear tuned-in and I could detect certain patterns and commonly grouped sounds. One word seemed to crop up everywhere; it sounded like *"ya'ni"* and I soon learned that it meant "meaning" or "that is to say" but that in fact it usually had no meaning at all but generally indicated a dysfluency much the same way we might habitually say "erm" or "uh". What I really needed was more vocabulary. Then I discovered that there were apparently four hundred words for lion and I became rather overawed until coming across a conversational dictionary which rather helpfully in the contents to the 1955 United States second edition included "New Phrases" such as those needed for travellers by car or using a camera. It was interesting to see that now Arabic had its own words for "air-raid shelter"; "anesthetic"[*sic*]; "gas mask" and "preventive war".

8

DISCOVERING DAMASCUS

The townes-men maske in silke and cloath of gold,
And every house is as a treasurie.

Christopher Marlowe - Tamburlaine, Pt 1, c.1587

It was just before dawn on Boxing Day morning when I was standing at the side of the road listening with concern to the howling of several dogs that seemed to have encircled me. I had put my rucksack down and picked up a couple of rocks which might serve as a defence and wished again that a car would pass soon and give me a lift into Amman as I wanted to catch an early *servees-taxi* to Damascus; preferably before I perished from frostbite or perhaps even dog-bite. I was about to make my first trip out of Jordan since arriving in September and was keenly looking forward to a brief visit to Syria. I planned to meet some Dutch volunteers who were working in the deaf school in Beirut along with the Brother Andrew who had made a brief visit there for the Christmas holiday and our rendezvous was to be the Grand Hotel in Umayyad Square. I knew little more than that it was easy to find as it overlooked the place where the authorities conducted public hangings. I wondered whether this got a mention in the hotel brochure as I at last piled into a beaten up Mercedes taxi with four other passengers heading north to the Syrian border.

The day was rather damp and grey, and had it not been for my excited anticipation at heading into unknown territory again, the journey would have been rather depressing. It was the middle of winter and the scenery was drab and muddy. As we approached the border town of Dera'a the flat stony desert we had been driving through for hours turned black as it became littered with what appeared to be volcanic rock. I could not recall a more desolate place. My mind was also full of stories, not all apocryphal I'm sure, of westerners who had visited this country and not returned. After all, it was run as a military dictatorship under President Hafez al-Assad, and there was certainly a large military presence at the border and tensions were high. Recent press reports stated that the government was being supplied with "squadrons" of military fighter aircraft including MIG-27s – Russia's most sophisticated, along with 75 T-12 tanks and an unspecified quantity of ground-to-ground and long range missiles, but that these planes were no match for the American supplied F-15s which the Israelis flew... I think this comment was meant to reassure the reader.

I was reminded of the colonial history of Syria by the rather quaintly stamped *"Pour les quinze jours"* on my entry visa – a legacy of the previous French influence. I would probably not be the last person to wonder whether I might remain in the country for fourteen or fifteen days, but it didn't seem the sort of country where one might usefully have an intellectual conversation with a border official on French etymology. The history of the Mandates interested me. This was yet another part of the world where our empires had defined the geography of nations through political motive rather than logical division. Clearly there were cultural differences between the peoples who were indigenous to this region and it must have been difficult to draw a line between them. I had already seen a diverse mix of ethnicities at the crossing point. There were Bedouin, looking like picture book Arabs in traditional dress; Palestinians in suits – the only outward acknowledgment of their heritage being their white head scarves and prayer beads - they were generally orthodox Sunni Muslims, although a significant proportion was Christian. I had seen several unusually blond types who must have been Circassians, a non-Arab Sunni Muslim minority who were originally refugees from the Caucasus who fled the Russian invaders in previous centuries. Most intriguing of all was a small group of men who were wearing on their heads a type of fez wrapped round in a white scarf. At first I thought they were priests of some kind but I later learned that they were members of a minority group called the Druze. They lived mainly in the mountainous parts of Lebanon and Syria and were very close-knit followers of a secretive monotheist religious sect who had managed to maintain their identity over nearly a thousand years. In part this was due to a strict bar on inter-marriage or any conversion from or to their religion. It may also have helped that in times of persecution a Druze was allowed to outwardly deny his faith if he believed his life was in danger. They played a prominent role in Syrian politics and were a potent force in the nationalist struggle against the French. It is certain that when the British and French were partitioning the region they would have been a vocal minority in the south of Syria, for the bulk of them lived in the Jebel al-Druze, a rugged mountainous region in the south of the country close to where the boundary line was to pass.

I had heard an interesting story from a diplomat working at the British embassy in Amman about why the Syrian-Jordanian border formed a perfectly straight boundary along most its length but at one point it diverted in such a way so as to incorporate the very small Druze settlement of Kirbet Aouad into the Syrian side. Apparently the surveyors were instructed to go to a point south of the village and form a right-angle triangle which would meet up with the original boundary line and which would incorporate within it the whole of the settlement. As told to me; wherever they positioned the apex of the right-angle the area enclosed by it omitted several houses on the edge of the village. There was some discussion about demolishing the offending houses when the French surveyor came up with a neat solution.... "It eez obviously not ze *right* angle!" ... and so they made it 95°.

It is entirely possible that this anecdote is true. To understand the story it is necessary to recount a little of the history of the British and French Mandates. The Franco-British Boundary Agreement (1920) contained the principles and defined the boundary in broad terms. It established a joint commission to settle the border and mark it on the ground (this was the commission which in 1923 transferred the Golan Heights from the British to the French Mandate). However, this commission again only defined the border in general terms and it wasn't until Britain and France signed a Protocol in Paris in 1931 that the detail was confirmed. The section of the border in question was defined in that Protocol as:

"...Section east of Nasib and Jaber. From the point specified above between Nasib and Jaber up to the meeting of the Trans-Jordan and Iraq frontier...

...The frontier will be indicated by landmarks placed at 3 kilometres 200 (that is two miles) to the North and parallel to the lines which join the centres of the places or localities mentioned above.

It is understood that, if the village of Kirbet Aouad or any part of this village were found to be south of the frontier line marked out as stated above, the frontier would bend to a point situated at sixty metres south and around the last group of houses at present existing; the junction with the general line being made east and west of the village by lines forming an angle of about 90 degrees with the point above indicated (60 metres south of the village) in such a way as to include in Druze territory all the inhabited part of this village as well as the territories situated in this angle reconnecting with the general line."[*]

Maps indicate that the present border between Syria and Jordan does indeed divert radically at only this point and form a small triangle, the acute angle of which is not quite 90°. It seems that the Druze, although a small minority, were indeed a force not to be overlooked.

Our taxi passed numerous military barracks and eventually arrived at a garage quite close to my destination. It was not yet lunchtime but wanting

---

[*] Source: International Boundary Study No. 94 – December 30, 1969 Jordan – Syria Boundary. The Geographer, Office of the Geographer Bureau of Intelligence and Research, US Department of State.

to dump my bag as quickly as possible and explore the local area I made my way to the "The Grand". It may have been grand once but a distinct seediness had since descended on this establishment. Still, the cockroaches in the room appeared harmless and the room rate suitably low. Changing some money at a nearby tobacconist I noticed a street vendor wearing yellow "marigolds" on his hands selling prickly pears, or *saber* as he was calling them, these were the delicious fruit of a cactus and the gloves were to protect his hands from the hundreds of minute spines which caused much irritation if touched. The narrow streets around the entrance to the *souk* were crowded with stalls and hundreds of items were for sale from fruit and tobacco to underwear and gold jewellery. I encountered no other Europeans on my exploration save for a pair of off-duty United Nations soldiers, possibly on a break from Lebanon.

By early evening, venturing with my Dutch companions deeper into the *souk,* we came upon the grand Umayyad mosque one of the largest and oldest in the world and a kind of St Paul's cathedral equivalent but with three minarets as well as a huge dome. As one of our party was a priest in clerical attire (including a long black beard) we nonchalantly entered the complex thinking we would not stand out in a great hall more than five hundred feet long. Everywhere were overlapping small carpets used as prayer mats; each one with a slightly different pattern and together presenting a very gaudy panorama. Inevitably we were accosted by an elderly Muslim cleric who introduced himself as the Imam, the leader of the prayers. We must have looked an odd group but we were made welcome and invited in to a small cell-like office. Before long I realised that English would not be understood – nor would Dutch for that matter, and as only one of us spoke Arabic conversation continued in French which fortunately I had studied at school.... though less fortunately, I had failed to excel at. The Imam's command of the language was excellent, by all accounts, but I was struggling. It wasn't long before we moved outside of my lexicon of formal greetings and salutations and moved on to subjects more metaphysical or theological. Conversation seemed to have gone on for hours when suddenly the Imam remembered that he had offered no refreshment and to his embarrassment explained that all he had available was a tin of honey and a teaspoon which he warmly offered round. Concerned not to offend, we all partook of the honey and wondered what would be the correct etiquette for passing it on: spoon in... or spoon out? If the latter: licked or wiped? I left the mosque with a feeling that I had experienced an evening of something quite unique, and convinced that it might have been a good idea to have paid more attention in my school French lessons. With our departure came an invitation to the Imam's home the following evening where he would be better able to offer us hospitality. This we all gladly accepted – how could we refuse?

Finding the address supplied was a challenge, especially as it was dark and the labyrinthine alleys of the *souk* were mostly unlit, but find it we eventually did. There was an ancient wooden door in one of the mud-rendered alley walls somewhere behind the mosque just like all the other ancient doors in this area. The alley had no rainwater gulley and was little more than a muddy stream of litter and building rubble. The walls were high and windowless and covered in places with graffiti in Arabic script. Anyone living here must live in complete poverty I thought. Of course I was wrong, as once through the door I came into a courtyard with ancient buildings on three sides, each having a timber balcony or gallery looking into the marbled yard with its central water feature - a picture postcard scene. The Imam and his family greeted us as we removed our shoes and were taken into a room full of cushions where we again sat and continued the previous evening's conversations, only this time the Imam treated us to delicious preserved apricots and endless cups of sweet tea while his family stayed discretely in a nearby room.

I was to return to the school in Jordan in two days so had time for only limited exploring in the old city, but I was lucky enough to be introduced to Deeb, a member of the local deaf club, who took me to his shoe shop on the north side of the great mosque. His father had made shoes here all his life and Deeb was following in the business, though now sold more imported items and repaired rather than made the shoes. Sadly there was no time to have a pair of leather shoes made for me. The cost would have been small but time was against me. I wondered whether I would ever get such a chance again. Deeb spoke good English and had learned how to lip-read which was a great advantage in the running of his business, though he recounted one awkward experience when a woman came into his shop one day covered from head to foot in the traditional black garb commonly worn in the country by Muslim women. He explained to her that he was deaf but that if she removed her head-covering so that he could see her mouth then he would be able to converse normally with her. As she did this her husband walked into the shop and a fierce argument ensued with Deeb only narrowly escaping a beating!

We made short excursion up to the Orthodox nunnery at Seydnaya (an ancient Syriac word in Aramaic dialect meaning "our lady" and "a place for hunting"). This convent was founded in the sixth century by the Byzantine Emperor Justinian the First and sat perched strategically on a rock outcrop on the edge of this small mountain town north of Damascus. Here was a pocket of Christians who had hung on against the pressures of the Muslim majority for hundreds of years. The citadel had been much visited during the time of the Crusades and the shrine was full of priceless icons including one supposedly painted by St Luke. For once the sun came out and I was treated to the memorable views which had drawn many earlier travellers; brown open fields dotted with the small white box-like houses of the local farmers, disappearing into a range of cotton wool capped hills beyond. This close to the Lebanese border I toyed for a while with the idea of returning with my companions via Beirut but quickly saw the flaw in this plan as I was not here for a holiday, but had responsibilities back at the school in Salt. I would have to await another opportunity should it arise. That evening, before going our separate ways, we enjoyed the delights of a meal at Ali Baba's Restaurant for the extravagant sum equivalent to £3 per person. (Extravagant, because I was receiving an allowance of only £2.50 a week at the time)

The return drive provided much more entertainment than the outward leg. Firstly, the rain had stopped, and secondly the taxi I was in comprised an enormous American saloon of some thirty year's vintage. I had noticed that whereas virtually every taxi in Jordan was a Mercedes often of the stretch-limo variety, in Damascus the driving population favoured a wide variety of old American makes although ancient Mercedes 190s and Peugeot 504s were also prevalent. It seemed this stemmed from a prohibition since the 1950s on people buying cars on the open market. Instead, the government bought thousands of cars each year and sold them to the people. In any particular year thousands of a single model might have been imported and made available. As new cars became too expensive to purchase, durable old cars became a valuable asset and were therefore passed from one generation to another each owner stamping their own individuality upon the vehicle, whether by installing a lurid green interior or non-standard accessories or even engines - originality not really being a concern. Necessity required inventiveness. My particular car appeared original, having outrageous fin-tailed wings and suspension that brought to mind sailing across the Bay of Biscay. Somewhere in the southern suburbs the driver encountered a traffic jam. Nothing was moving in either direction, perhaps because of an accident up ahead, a common enough occurrence given that the likelihood of it happening was entirely at the will of *Allah* and apparently unconnected to events of a more terrestrial nature. After brief consultation with my fellow passengers in which the aforementioned deity was frequently cited, our driver decided to turn off the road and go around the obstacle; an ambitious manoeuvre given the car's quirky suspension and the nine inch high curb. Nevertheless, it was accomplished with panache and a grinding of metal. Henceforth we were to proceed on our journey making a noise like a tank, leading me to believe that part of the exhaust system might have been left behind adding to the junk already clogging the highway. Clearly unperturbed, and without any intention of stopping to inspect the damage, our driver brought us to the border crossing. Unexpectedly this provided further entertainment as we drove over the obligatory inspection pit occupied by a soldier whose job it was to conduct a search of the underside of the vehicle looking for contraband or perhaps weapons. After a few seconds the soldier banged on the underside of the car to indicate that he had completed his search and we might proceed. However despite much revving and rocking forward we remained stuck over the pit. The more the engine was revved the more the soldier was suffocating from the fumes of the broken exhaust and the more he banged on the car. Luckily for him one of his colleagues suggested that it might be easier if we reversed off. Adopting what was clearly a favoured style our driver again chose not to stop and investigate and we sailed quickly through the border post and onto the next town where at a small concrete shack a whole new exhaust system was fabricated by a teenage youth in a little over an hour. It occurred to me later that the taxi would be repeating this journey several times a day and so time was very much of the essence. Of course this did not increase my confidence in the driver.

9

WANDERINGS IN THE WEST BANK

"Here we are in the holy land of Israel – a Mecca for tourists"

David Vine - Private Eye Magazine, 1980

Over the centuries many people have written weighty books and respected academic works on the subject of Palestine and Israel including Edward Gibbon who in his lengthy account of the Rise and Fall of the Roman Empire expressed this somewhat laconic view: *"Palestine ... a territory scarcely superior to Wales, either in fertility or extent."* although from this it is not at all clear whether he had visited the area. Clearly what I needed was a more objective view and as I had decided to spend a few days of my Easter leave in an exploration of Israel, or occupied West Bank as the Jordanian authorities insisted on calling it, I felt I could obtain one.

The necessary precursor to any visit to the occupied territory was a visit to the relevant Ministries in Amman to obtain a permit. This was not the same as a visa, as of course one would not be necessary given that the West Bank of the Jordan was still Jordanian territory and simply under Israeli military administration, and so just comprised an informal looking piece of paper. It was necessary to flit between the Ministries of Information, Interior and Defence, and eventually after several days, armed with this document and on this occasion accompanied by John, the Project Trust volunteer who was working at the German Theodore Schneller School in Amman, I set off from Salt to hitch-hike down into the Jordan Valley along the old Jerusalem Road. Pausing at the marker indicating sea level we duly took each other's photograph with the view of the valley floor some way below and behind us, much as every independent traveller passing that way must have done since the invention of the Kodak Instamatic camera. The scene was surreal and we carried on winding downwards for sometime before reaching the valley bottom where amongst small fruit plantations we eventually arrived after only thirty-three miles at the police post at the eastern end of the bridge over the River Jordan. This formed the crossing point five miles east of Jericho (and some 895ft below sea level). The bridge, still called the Allenby Bridge by Israelis, although it was also known as Al-Karameh Bridge to Palestinian Arabs and the King Hussein Bridge to Jordanians, was originally built by General Allenby in 1918 upon the remnants of an old Ottoman structure. The present bridge comprised a flimsy looking temporary structure rather like a World War II "Bailey Bridge" erected in 1968 to replace one destroyed in the Six-Day War, which itself replaced one blown up in 1946. I was aware of another bridge some thirty miles to the north at Damia (known to the Israelis as Adam Bridge) although no-one I spoke to could tell me much about it other than it was possibly in occasional use for commercial and agricultural transport but was probably out of bounds to foreigners. At the Ministry in Amman there had been no mention of Damia Bridge and as no-one had asked which route we proposed to follow we thought it safer to follow the more conventional one. Whether we could have crossed further north I never discovered, but apparently the crossing remained in use right up to 1991. There had been two further bridges across the Jordan; the King Abdullah Bridge to the south which had not been rebuilt since the 1967 conflict, and one which crossed the river into the Golan Heights (now occupied Syrian territory) which was similarly disused. I had spent ages studying my Jordanian Tourist Ministry map, compiled by the Ministry of Lands and Surveys in 1962. It showed the full extent of the country prior to the loss of the West Bank and was a fascinating historical document. Not only did it depict the West Bank towns in Arabic with English translations; extending from Hebron in the south to Jenin in the north, but it showed just how close the land extended in the west towards the Mediterranean – only 9 miles away - and included the border with Israel running straight through Jerusalem.

Because of the particular status of the West Bank the Jordanian authorities would not permit foreigners to exit from their territory at the Allenby Bridge. This meant that those wishing to leave Jordan were required to first return across the bridge, and then depart from one of the international departure points such as the airport in Amman. Similarly, the Jordanians would not allow any foreigner to enter the country from this point even if they possessed a valid Jordanian visa. It was intriguing therefore to find on the other side of the bridge that the Israelis did treat this as an international entry point and that one step into the West Bank was one step into Israel proper for no further restrictions or crossings were to be encountered which might prevent one's access to the whole of that country. The immigration desk would have happily stamped our passports had we not insisted against this, and instead they stamped our "Registration of Entry/Exit" forms, in this way we would be allowed back into Jordan with no evidence in our passports that we had in fact visited Israel. We had been warned that in such an eventuality a flight to Cyprus would be required in order to obtain a new clean passport and fresh entry visa. Whether or not this was true John and I had the neither inclination nor funds to test the process. This mechanism struck me as odd, as the Jordanian authorities were aware of what happened at the border crossing and knew that a traveller had probably been to Israel i.e. travelled through the country's original West Bank boundaries, but it presumably allowed them to continue with the delusion that Israel did not really exist.

No private transport was allowed over the bridge although there was a seemingly continuous stream of trucks carrying great limestone boulders from quarries near Hebron and farm produce in wooden crates from Gaza and other parts of the West Bank, all of whom swapped over their Israeli licence plates for Jordanian ones and proceeded on up the road the 36 miles to Amman. I was told that the reason wooden crates were used was because Jordan did not allow the import of Israeli goods and banned cardboard boxes which were made in that country. At the immigration checkpoint different rules applied for Jordanians and Palestinians due to the "open bridge" policy implemented in 1967 by Israel which provided a unique arrangement for residents crossing between two territories still officially at war. Those residents of Judea, Samaria, the Gaza Strip and East Jerusalem were allowed to cross to Jordan to continue to export their agricultural produce such as Jaffa oranges as they had done before the war. No Israelis or Israeli Arabs were allowed across the bridge, a situation which continued up until 1991. I did know of one private car which had made the crossing; this belonged to the Bishop of Jerusalem, his car, resplendent with its pale blue Israeli licence plate, arrived one morning on a visit to the Institute in Salt – to my amazement completely without bullet holes or smashed windscreen!

There were stringent checks on us as we passed through the Israeli checkpoint. I was struck by how modern and how efficient everything seemed. The air-conditioning worked and even the number of women in army uniform was remarkable, something not seen in Jordan. Everything we had in our rucksacks was unpacked and our shoes X-rayed. I even had the inside of my camera checked although luckily I had been warned that this might happen and had not inserted a film. These checks seemed officious and gave an indication of the high level of security we were to encounter during our brief stay in the country. Curiously, part way through the process a loud siren sounded and all the Israeli officials stopped what they were doing and stood to attention. This struck me as rather surreal and I wondered if this was perhaps part of some daily ritual like the Muslim's call to prayer – there was no explanation or even acknowledgement of this interruption to proceedings. We said goodbye to the luxurious air-conditioning and left the building to look for a taxi to take us the remaining 26 miles up to Jerusalem.

Crossing over the narrow waters of the Jordan I had not only moved from one culture to another, I had in effect crossed from one age to another and into a different world – at least that is how it appeared when in Israeli controlled space. Initially though, the small Arab hamlets and villages we passed on our climb up towards Jerusalem looked exactly like those we'd left on the eastern side; poor, haphazardly constructed of bare concrete blocks and full of brightly clad young children with their mothers in the traditional black garb of Muslim women, playing in the dirt outside their homes and shouting at every passing car. There was little sign of the spread of Jewish settlements until we reached the outskirts of Jerusalem.

Entering the Old City from Jericho I had only an imperfect view of the extent of the modern Israeli developments which had on three sides vastly increased its size since 1948. All around were the features of ancient and biblical times dominated by the Dome of the Rock – a site of great significance to Christians, Muslims and Jews alike. At sundown I found myself at the Western Wall below the Dome where a military ceremony was underway. Someone explained that today was *Yom Hazikaron* – Memorial Day for the Fallen Soldiers. This probably accounted for the siren at lunchtime I thought. There was much marching up and down and raising of flags after which access was again granted for the devout Jews wishing to pray at the wall. Whilst it was fascinating to watch their praying and inserting of little pieces of paper into the cracks in the stonework on which they had written prayers, it was time to find a bed for the night and so John and I headed to the Armenian hostel on the Via Dolorosa in the Armenian quarter of the Old City. We had heard that this was cheap but clean accommodation and we were keen to soak up the ambience of the ancient city. After enjoying a refreshingly cold shower in the austere dormitory accommodation of the hostel, and entrusting our rucksacks to the care of a heavily bearded and very fierce-looking cat, presumably Armenian, we went out to explore. I had encountered only a handful of tourists during my months in Jordan but knew that I might expect to see many in this ancient city and so shrugging off the backpack of an explorer I reconciled myself to slipping on the mantle of a tourist for a couple of days and sharpened my elbows in order to secure the most advantageous positions to take the obligatory tourist photographs. I had not however expected to find myself in the middle of a crowd of thousands of people of all ages gaily moving around the streets hitting each other over the head with plastic hammers! Needless to say I acquired one myself quite quickly and entered into the spirit of things, even attempting to join in with some of the folk dances which appeared to be taking place spontaneously in every street. After a while John thought it worthwhile establishing what the particular occasion was; it seemed odd to celebrate Remembrance Day in such a way. Finding a friendly looking little old lady with a pooch in her arms he enquired. "We are celebrating independence" she shouted. "From whom?" asked John (rather naively as it happened...) "From YOU!" came the emphatic reply. Thereafter, we went about with a little more circumspection and avoided any conversations with the locals which might invite reference to 1948. *Yom Ha-Atzmaut*, the Israeli Independence Day, had started a few minutes after sundown. The linking with *Yom Hazikaron* was explained in that the state owed its very existence to the soldiers who sacrificed their lives for it. Celebrations would extend through the night and into the next day which was designated a public holiday. After a while we tired of the crowds. I also had an odd feeling about sharing in these particularly nationalist celebrations; strangely, a feeling I encountered in reverse just a few years later as a student when a friend from my days in Guernsey came to my house to cook a meal to celebrate "Liberation Day" on the 9th May. My flatmate Heinrich enquired without thinking from whom had she had been liberated...?

Eight weeks previously the Israeli government had decided that it should convert the local currency from Israeli pounds to *shekels*. The choice of name may have had something to do with nationalism but the reason behind it was to do with economic inflation. The exchange rate was ten pounds for one *shekel*. Local tradesmen were still getting to grips with this change, made harder by the fact that the new bank notes were almost identical to the old ones, with only the number in words and symbols differing between the old and the new notes. This was a major hazard for the unwary. Numerous times when handing over a ten *shekel* note I was proffered the change for a ten pound one! Within five years these *shekels* were to be themselves replaced by new *shekels* at a rate of one thousand to one. The Jerusalem Post, which was helpfully published in English, reported that inflation for the month of April was 10.2% having risen from 5.11% the previous month. This may sound awful, but put into annual terms it was horrific - over the previous twelve months inflation had hit 123.48% and was set to continue rising. The price of bread went up almost every day I was in the country, but as my expenditure was very low I was not really aware of it, but it must have made life very difficult for the locals – not all of whom were wealthy and could afford posh cars and motorcycles.   Telephone boxes worked by using tokens whose cost also conveniently went up almost daily.   There was a very noticeable wealth gap between the Jewish population and the Palestinians as I was to discover when I left Jerusalem to head up through the occupied West Bank through Nablus and Jenin towards Lake Tiberias.   Pausing to take tea at various roadside shops I felt as though at home in Jordan again.   After all, this was the homeland of many of the deaf children I had left back at the school and any one of their relatives could have been serving me my tea.

With a brief stop at Nazareth – because it was there – we eventually arrived at the town of Tiberias on the western shore of Lake Tiberias, or the Sea of Galilee as it was known by many.   Immediately I was struck by the western style and appearance of the town.   Teenage girls clad in only shorts and tee-shirts travelled on the back of their boyfriends' motorbikes.   What decadence it seemed; after living for more than six months in an Arab country I felt a shudder of culture shock come over me – at least I think that's what it was.   We collected a town map from the Tourist Information Office and set off to find the "Tirat Ha-Agam" hostel.   As we made our way to the lakeside for a swim I couldn't help notice that of all the many beaches labelled on this map one was identified as Gay Beach – this was clearly a more liberal country than I thought – I didn't recall any such facility back in the UK, and I wondered how the more traditional Arabs might view this; although not many of them were apparent in this town.   It may have been a misprint of course, as the English found on maps I had seen did tend to be rather idiosyncratic, although what it could have been a misprint for left me puzzled.   At the hostel we encountered the first English people of our age either of us had met in months.   These were two long-haired and extremely tanned guys from Uxbridge called Baz and Mick.   It was difficult to relate to their experiences as they had been many months in Israel having a good time and travelling between various *kibbutzim*, such a different world from that found only a few miles away across the valley.   One useful tip I did pick up though, was how to blag a stay at a *kibbutz* and secure free accommodation and meals, and I intended to try this out when we headed over to the west of the country in a day or so.

We hitch-hiked all the time, as apart from being a cheap and easy way to travel it was an opportunity to meet a variety of people and learn something of life in Israel. Just about every Israeli we encountered spoke English, and those who didn't, spoke Arabic. John's command of Arabic was superior to my own as the children he was working with were not deaf and he needed the language to be able to converse with them, whereas I primarily relied upon sign language back at the school. Nevertheless we could both make ourselves understood when necessary in whichever language. The important thing to remember when hitch-hiking was never to use one's thumb as apparently this was considered most rude. Clearly hitch-hiking had a language of its own. We found that we were considered an oddity by those we met for we did not behave like most tourists who travelled in large groups, wielding enormous cameras at all and sundry. I tried to explain that these were mainly rich American tourists and that we were simply travellers - neither of us flush with money, and the longer we could make our cash last, the further we could travel. The road out of Tiberias took us through Rosh Pinna, one of the oldest Zionist settlements in Israel. We decided not to stop at the youth hostel there as our lift was a good one heading right across to the coast and we felt the urge to move on particularly given our tight schedule. One of the drawbacks of hitch-hiking (and there are of course several) is that one cannot usually dictate the route or speed, nor the frequency and location of stops, so this potentially interesting village was passed like so many other places on our journey. Occasionally one is offered the opportunity to decide these things, which is the time to be suspicious and look for any early exit. After brief halts at Akko and Haifa were we managed a little sight-seeing we found ourselves deposited from our last lift of the day in the road outside a *kibbutz* which proclaimed itself to be called Dalia. Now was the time to see if we could blag our way in.

The technique recommended was surprisingly simple and involved asking at the gate whether our alleged friend Samuel from Manchester who was working as a volunteer was able to come and greet us. We were invited in to go and look for him in the refectory as it was supper time. Clearly this *kibbutz* was large enough for no-one to know the identity of all of the volunteers... Joining the food queue we quickly made friends with some English volunteers and in a matter of moments had secured the promise of some space on a floor in one of the chalets. Neither of us had any experience of *kibbutzim* and did not know what to expect, but in our very short stay we were made welcome and experienced the generosity of all those we encountered in this community. Dalia *kibbutz* turned out to be quite well established. It had been founded from the combination of two other *kibbutzim* in 1939 by farmers who had immigrated from Romania and Germany in 1933. Apparently at that time the site comprised just stones and a single fig tree and was not suited to agriculture so the settlers started a blacksmiths and also began making soap. Eventually an abundant water supply was discovered by which time the *kibbutz* members were successfully making water-meters and detergent.

The route back to Jerusalem took us via Tel Aviv, a totally western-styled city (previously known as Jaffa) and a place neither of us wanted to hang around in. Returning to the Armenian hostel in Jerusalem we paid our respects to the cat and noted that bread had again risen in price (though not in substance). Strangely, despite our fascinating tour, neither of us was too sorry to be leaving this ancient land full of antiquity – and tourists. It was a mental strain after the slower pace of Jordanian life. Here also, was a country of stark contrasts: everywhere people in military uniform side by side with the civilian population; well-dressed women in western fashions alongside those in traditional Palestinian garb; smart new vans with impatient drivers tooting their way through crowds and around over-laden donkeys led by bent old men; flocks of pigeons let out for their daily exercise over-flown by noisy military aircraft; roofs bristling with television aerials and solar water heaters obscuring views of ancient minarets and towers; modern blocks of city flats besides modest rural dwellings – they were everywhere, and served to create differences between the peoples who could lay equal claim to much of this land. To me it felt unsettling to be there, having spent so many months living and working in the comparatively poor town of Salt with many children who were either refugees themselves, or children of those whose families were originally from the Arab towns now under Israeli control. This wasn't so much because of the politics of the situation, nor was it out of any sense of guilt as a Briton whose forebears had been largely responsible for creating some of these problems; it was simply because I had grown accustomed to a more simple life and one less spoilt by obviously western trends and fashions. How long this situation might remain in Jordan I had no way to tell, but I was keen to return to Salt. That said, both John and I fully intended to return and see more of the sights of Israel should we ever have sufficient free time or find the pace of life in Jordan just too slow.

After completing formalities at the Allenby Bridge we caught the last bus across the hundred yards or so separating the two country's border controls and arrived back in what was most definitely Jordan. We had a whole afternoon to fill and as the journey back to Salt should only take a couple of hours or so we decided to go and visit the Dead Sea, just a little way to the south of us. An obliging farmer offered a lift in the back of his Toyota pick-up and we were deposited at a remote spot where there may once have been a "resort". The clue was in the presence of a block of two showers on a concrete base. These weren't connected to any water supply we could detect, and nor were they anywhere near the shore. It seemed that here was first-hand evidence of the shrinking of the Sea. When we found the water, more than a hundred yards further west, much to my surprise there were large waves rolling into the beach – some nearly two feet high. I had only seen tourist pictures of the Dead Sea and these all depicted people floating on top of a mirror of water, it hadn't occurred to me that it might be affected by wind and weather. Undeterred, we both waded in only to be bowled over by the first wave as it swept our legs from under us. Once prone in the water I was able to paddle out some distance, and turning to face the shore, lined myself up in readiness to surf in on the next big wave. Together John and I hurtled into the beach body-surfing on the very top of the water. This provided an exhilarating five minutes until inevitably I splashed some water in my face and was then blinded by the saturated saline solution until I could rinse my eyes clean with my water bottle back on the beach. After this we decided it was time to set off home and creaking in a layer of salt under our clothes we walked uncomfortably in the humid heat of the late afternoon back along the track in search of what we hoped would be the last lift of the day.

10

JORDAN EXPLORED

Go, wash thyself in Jordan — go, wash thee and be clean!
Nay, not for any Prophet will I plunge a toe therein!
For the banks of curious Jordan are parcelled into sites,
Commanded and embellished and patrolled by Israelites.

Rudyard Kipling – "Naaman's Song", Limits and Renewals, 1932

There was an English couple from Nottingham living in Amman who had got to know of the Institute in its early days and had been very supportive of its work. They had the idea after the birth of their first child that it might be auspicious to have him christened in the River Jordan and so asked Brother Andrew if he would officiate. At that time the river formed the border between two nations officially at war and access along its entire length was forbidden; not even from the Israeli side was this allowed. There had been occasional armed incursions across the border and whilst symbolic baptisms might have been common in pre-1967 days they were unheard of at this time. Tourists were comparatively few in any event. Those with official tour groups were restricted to the key historic sites of Amman, Petra, Jerash, Kerak and Aqaba while those with more independent inclinations were restricted by the parochial knowledge of their chosen taxi driver – and the language barrier – hire cars were rare, and the independent traveller could easily find themselves in difficulty without an off-road vehicle or adequate local knowledge. As it happened Brother Andrew knew of a site where the river forked and a small island had been formed having both banks of its eastern side technically in Jordan. We would aim for this spot, relying simply on a permit to be in the general area obtained from the officials in Salt and as usual on the "protective cloak" afforded by the clerical garb of an Anglican priest. Excited more by the prospect of accessing a part of the Jordan Valley I would never otherwise get to see than by the prospect of a christening, I dressed in a clean pair of jeans, brushed up my "desert wellies" and merrily entered into the spirit of the occasion. John was also invited from the Schneller School, which added to the sense of adventure.

The chosen site was jungle-like in that the vegetation which had at one time been cultivated, presumably as part of a now dispossessed family's smallholding, was wildly overgrown. There were banana trees on the island though now oleanders and scrub had subsumed most of the river's banks. Orange trees were set back from the water's edge still enjoying the free irrigation of the ancient waters. The service was a simple affair with the child being held by his mother, while various other participants stood knee deep in the flowing water while Brother Andrew intoned the necessary liturgy with a degree of improvisation which suited the surroundings. Meanwhile I was happily taking photographs up to the point that I was called upon to take a prayer book to the officiant. There was no time to take off my boots and roll up my trousers as the others had done, so I blithely waded straight in. The service was short and the child seemed none the worse for his total immersion, but before we adjourned for the planned picnic we had prepared it seemed only natural that we should all take a swim in the river. I could not help but imagine the reaction if the christening had been in church at home and the congregation had then all pulled on their costumes and dived into the font.

As it happened this was not my first excursion down to the river, a previous outing with some of the school children had taken place earlier in the year. On that occasion we had planned a barbeque at the side of the Yarmouk River to the north, one of three tributaries which feed the Jordan and rising on Mount Herman in the Anti-Lebanon mountain range; its summit the highest point in Syria. The course of the river forms in part the border between Jordan, Syria and Israel on the edge of the disputed Golan Heights and was another very sensitive area from which the general population was prohibited.[*]

Our route from Salt was north along the Jordan Valley driving within a stone's throw of Lake Galilee (Tiberias). Mount Tarbor near Nazareth was clearly visible on our left as we passed the few settlements on our route; in fact I saw more Israeli *kibbutzim* than Jordanian villages. The hills were mostly barren and here and there were areas fenced off with single-wire strands from which hung metal signs depicting the skull and cross-bones suggesting that the land was mined. Whether the local goats knew this wasn't clear as they continued to forage regardless of the obstacles. The Yarmouk Valley basin itself was green and obviously very fertile but was clearly not being actively farmed. As we travelled further up river an abandoned village came into sight on the inside of a deep meander. Over on the opposite bank its small mosque was still visible with trees growing out of houses and roads which had grassed over indicating that parts of this area had not been visited for a good many years. Nearby were the signs of a former railway line built by the Ottomans suggesting that this may have once been an important town. The line emerged from a tunnel before criss-crossing from bank to bank over box-girder bridges, one of which I noticed appeared to have been blown up. There was no way of telling

---

[*] The Yarmouk's waters are considerably reduced today by the presence of the al-Wehda dam constructed jointly by Jordan and Syria. Water extraction is now a contentious issue in this area but in 1980 the river was fast flowing and there had been little or no development of the land within its catchment since before the 1974 ceasefire; restrictions on access and lack of amenity making this impossible at the time.

whether this had been part of some Arab or Israeli action in the recent past, or the relic of an engagement between forces led by T. E. Lawrence against the Turks; I liked to think the latter. Eventually we crunched the vehicles down a rocky track right onto a sheltered pebbled beach which looked suitable to form a picnic area for the afternoon. We could have been beside any river except for the dominating feature of the high barbed-wire fence running all along the top of the steep bluff above the opposite bank intermittently reinforced by tall machine gun towers. I couldn't see if these were manned but it was probably the case and also safe to assume that the fortifications we had passed on the way down were likewise occupied by the opposing Jordanian troops. As we waited for the fire to die down enough for cooking I decided to go for a swim, but finding the water too fast flowing made for the opposite bank under the cliff. Some of the older boys followed me before I realised that this was not the wisest of moves given that I had technically crossed the border presumably under the gaze of countless binoculars. Not wishing to alarm the children I quickly led them back across to the shallows on the Jordanian side.

It wasn't long before the sun dropped low enough to bring on an early dusk in the gorge and we made ready to leave as the journey back would be long and slow especially as it would be dark before we found our way onto a proper road. Back-tracking the way we had come we eventually returned to something resembling a road and were just gathering speed when two soldiers leapt out of the shadows in front of the Chevrolet bringing it to sudden halt. Very politely they explained that the way was now closed as it had been booby-trapped for the night and would we like to turn around and proceed in the opposite direction! I remember that we argued that we had many tired children on board and that the other way would add several hours to our journey – I'm not sure whether we wanted to give the impression that the children were somehow impervious to mines, or whether we thought that the claim was just a ruse by the soldiers to extract some *baksheesh*. However we eventually gave way to the inevitable and turned around. This was the most exciting part of the day for some of the children who occupied themselves on the drive home embellishing the story as best they could in the dark so as to be able to impress their friends back at the school.

Early in January we were paid a brief visit by a former volunteer, Martin who had previously been a volunteer with Project Trust in South Africa and was helping Father Andeweg out in Beirut. His visit happened to coincide with one of my days off and we decided to go and visit Aqaba and try and get a swim in the Red Sea, a round trip of nearly 500 miles. Everyone thought we were mad – especially as it had just started snowing, nevertheless undaunted we wanted to give it a go. To give ourselves a little head start we decided to hitch up to Amman the evening before, sleeping on the floor at a friend's house, and then travel down the Desert Highway early the next morning. To our amazement we were lucky with our lifts and arrived in Aqaba well before midday having spent only four hours hitchhiking. A short ride out further south along the road towards Saudi found us on a beach flaked out in the bright January sun. I'd heard that the coral was spectacular along this coast, but without any snorkelling equipment I wasn't able to enjoy it. Anyway, I was so pleased at having arrived in such a short time that nothing could take the shine off the day! Having swum enough and bored with lying around doing nothing we headed back into town to see if we could obtain a permit to travel homeward by a different route along Wadi Araba.

A permit would be needed to travel up Wadi Araba as the road ran beside the Israeli border right up to the Dead Sea and was in a restricted area. I knew from enquiry that the necessary permission might be hard to obtain but we both thought it worth a go as few people had travelled this road which was just a track in places and it sounded quite exciting. Asking the first policeman that we met where we might obtain permission he directed us to the secret police, known as the *mukhabarat*. To say he directed us is a little misleading as he had no idea where they could be found – obviously they were very secret. The next policeman we encountered pointed at an ice cream kiosk beside the beach. With low expectations we approached it thinking we could at least buy an ice cream before starting back up the Desert Highway. To my amazement the vendor inside said that he could provide us with the necessary permit and requested to see our passports! Some few minutes later we left the kiosk with an official looking form covered in Arabic script which allegedly proclaimed our permission to travel in the restricted area. As it had cost nothing I was inclined to believe its authenticity; for if the ice cream seller had simply been opportunistic surely he would have demanded a fee? Later back in Salt I had its authenticity confirmed – it had been signed by a high-ranking officer. I imagined that like me the man was having a day off and was perhaps helping a friend out on the beach... though I was still puzzled as to why he might take a full set of official forms with him.

By now it was 5pm and already late to be starting back for home. There was just time to write a couple of postcards and drop them in at the central post office as we walked up to the junction north of the town where the routes split. At this point my heart sank. I knew that the road was a track in some places but had not expected it to start as one. After about an hour we decided to cut our losses and head back up to Amman the way we had come for there had been no vehicle going in our intended direction. It was obviously too late in the day and as I had to return for work the next morning I couldn't go back and sleep on the beach and try again the next day when there might be more chance of a lift.

Our hitching started off well, and soon we thought that our luck of the morning would be repeated. At one point a small van stopped to pick us up. The driver and his passenger were happy to give us a lift if only we did not mind sitting in the back of the van. As it was now dark and we had a very long way to go we were not keen to refuse a lift, and so quickly hopped in amongst sacks of pistachio nuts. After the doors were slammed shut it dawned on me that we were completely trapped in total darkness in the back of a van entirely in the hands of two men we didn't know, at night, somewhere in the middle of the desert – probably not the wisest lift I had accepted. My consolation was that I was with Martin, and whilst he was probably as skinny as me, the two of us could put up a good fight – and I had my Swiss Army knife of course, given to me by one of the sailors on the Clan Graham. After a while we started to feel very hungry and using the knife I opened one of the sacks and we shared handfuls of delicious pistachio nuts, suddenly remembering that we'd hardly eaten all day. It seemed like we had been cooped up for several hours as the van made its way up the tarmac of the highway when suddenly we lurched back and forwards as the vehicle turned off the road and made its way across potholes and ruts before grinding to a halt in complete silence. We both thought "this is it!" and braced ourselves to leap out of the van as soon as the rear doors were opened and run as fast as possible back up to the main road. Instead, as the door was opened I saw the fluorescent lights of a roadside cafe and suddenly realised that we had merely stopped because our driver and his mate wanted to eat. To our embarrassment, for we had stuffed ourselves full with pistachios the evidence for which was littered across the van's floor, they even bought us dinner. True Arab hospitality.

Our journey continued uneventfully after that and we did manage to complete the round trip in under twenty-four hours. I learned many months later that the postcards which I had posted in Aqaba also achieved a remarkable journey; both arriving at their destinations in England the very next morning which must have been a record.

The countryside around the town of Salt was not short of spectacular scenery too and would have made an ideal subject for a set of picture postcards, with its rolling hills and spectacular views across the Jordan Valley to the hills surrounding Jerusalem. As a special treat I would sometimes be invited by the Swiss family to join them on an evening picnic on one of the nearby hills where the best views could be obtained. It was important to have a break from the intense life at the Institute and these occasional picnics were the precious private time that the family were able to make for themselves. Living on the job as they did meant that they were never really off duty – there was always some burst pipe to mend, a child who had injured themselves, some administrative problem to worry about or simply preparation required for the next day. On these occasions we would stop in the town and purchase a couple of spatchcock chickens which had already been coated with *zata* (a delicious mixture of herbs and spices) and a bag of fresh *khobis* baked that evening, and if I was invited, there would always be a cold bottle of Amstel beer (locally brewed in Amman). We would drive up to their favourite hill and find a suitable terrace upon which to picnic amongst the clumps of wild thyme and chirping crickets. From here I could look out west and see the brown rolling hills disappear below and flatten out into the brown valley floor. Snaking down the middle of the valley was the green serpent marking the banks of the Jordan and the irrigated orange groves on either side. More than ten miles distant I could just make out the individual rolling hills rising to form the western edge of the great rift valley, and as the sun sank to the horizon breaking through the haze it was possible to make out the minarets and other structures of Jerusalem silhouetted against the enlarged red orb and to imagine the evening call to prayer drifting across on the still air.

This was a magical spot and on more than one occasion when one of the other volunteers was invited we'd ask to be left at the site and collected again in the early morning. There was something special about lying on one's unrolled sleeping bag on a moonless night and watching the sky getting darker with the sinking sun and then the appearance of millions of stars and constellations in some of the darkest sky I can recall. The lights from the ground below in the valley bottom were like small torches flickering with weak batteries, the absence of towns, street lights and only minimal traffic making the skies darker. Only the lights of the ancient city opposite gave a faint glow. Occasionally flares would be launched along the line of the border as one side or other chose to keep their opponent on their toes, or perhaps they were triggered automatically... it was fun to speculate, just as it was fun to imagine that the many satellites which we could see passing over head in low orbit were all spying on the ground below... or perhaps us.

It could cool down considerably at night and a sleeping bag was a welcome accessory. Mine was an old green cotton affair, much patched but still serviceable. It was neither waterproof nor particularly warm – which didn't matter much here; what was significant was its colour. It seemed that I must have been the only green object for miles around for when I woke up one morning on the hard earth of the terrace and peered cautiously out from within the loosely tied neck I found I was surrounded by wild tortoises – all towering above me, and all nibbling at the green cloth of my sleeping bag inches from my face. Of course once I sat up I had things back in perspective, but the image of those "attacking" wild tortoises remains vivid to this day.

Inevitably at some point we were going to have to take the school children on a desert expedition to sample the wild and seemingly inhospitable sands in the east of the country. Only a few of the children came from Bedouin tribes as many had grown up in refugee camps in families which had been displaced or fled from the rural villages of Palestine. The desert in eastern Jordan was nothing like the fertile valleys and plains of these populous areas, it was a vast flat stony expanse without roads and few distinguishing features, as unfamiliar to most of the children as it was to me.

The planned trip required more vehicles than we normally had at our disposal but we were fortunate to be lent two VW mini buses to augment our two Chevrolets (one newly repaired after the ski-jump incident) and a Peugeot estate car. All were packed with sufficient food and water to last fifty-five children and twenty-five adults for a day –"packed" being the key word here. Our first stop of the day was at the small oasis of Azraq 50 miles east of Amman where the black and quite grim basalt of the lava country ended and the rolling desert began. We had a quick look at the black basalt fort of Lawrence of Arabia fame (from his headquarters here he launched his attack on Aqaba – I would have thought he might have chosen somewhere a little closer) and then had our barbeque beside the pools which formed the oasis proper. Here were the ubiquitous palms of my imagination. At Azraq the road ended and our drive on to Qasr al Amra followed a well-used dirt track. Here was a small but beautiful building with its internal walls adorned with frescoes suggesting that the surrounding land had not always been stony desert when this hunting lodge had been constructed over a thousand years before.

The sun was beginning to set as we headed on to Qasr al Kharanah. Our way was marked by large concrete cairn-like structures regularly placed so that not even in the thickest of sandstorms should the traveller stray from the route. Our stop at this fort was brief as the caretaker had already closed down for the night which was a pity as its impressive four-square walls pierced with arrow slits and its four round corner towers and single small entrance indicated that this had been a true defensive structure. Its strategic importance was not immediately apparent; it was obviously sited where many desert tracks met, but whether these were made before the fort or were formed because of its presence was not clear. Not far from the fort we came across a very large lizard of about three feet in length and stopped to take a clearer look. There are apparently fifty-six species of lizards in Jordan the largest of which is the delightfully named *varanus griseus*. None of us was brave enough to go too close save for Joshua who unhesitatingly stepped up to give it a prod with his artificial leg. Whether this particular specimen was indeed a desert monitor I don't know, but it seems likely.

By now the sun had completely disappeared and we commenced the final leg of our journey with little to guide us other than the stars for there was no longer any obvious track to follow. Given our location east and just south of Amman we decided to head directly west keeping the pole star on our right shoulder. Hitherto we had been driving in line astern, but visibility was much reduced at night by the dust thrown up by the vehicle in front and we had switched to line abreast as far as possible. I was riding "shotgun" in the big Chevrolet Suburban in the middle of the convoy, its big 5.7 litre V8 engine making crossing the terrain seem almost effortless, and my primary job was to periodically climb out of the window grabbing hold of the roof-rack and try to count the number of sets of headlights to ensure we were all still together. As a subsidiary role I was to also try and gauge the depth of some of the ravine-like hollows we were traversing – preferable before we crossed them. I was doing alright with the first job but next to useless with the second, and the children in the rear seats were continually hitting their heads on the ceiling as they were thrown up into the air. Suddenly I realised that we were one set of headlights short. Having alerted my driver we sped ahead and swung round in an arc so we could face the following vehicles and signal a halt. It quickly became apparent that we were without Joshua and a dozen children in the old Chevrolet and having the only four-wheel drive vehicle in the group it fell to us to backtrack and seek him out. We thought this should be easy as previously when one of our party had a puncture and dropped out of line we found them quickly by their headlights, but this time there was no sign. Eventually after nearly half an hour of driving we found them; they had an electrical fault which had cut out all power including lights and Joshua was busy trying to fix the problem. He looked like a ghost, as did all the children, for they were all covered with a fine grey dust from head to toes, only their teeth and the whites of their eyes reflecting in our headlights. Soon fixed, we were back on the move again and I think all of us were greatly relieved when we saw the lights on the main desert highway leading to Amman. The children nearly fell asleep in the showers that night when we eventually got back to Salt. They had been driven through the desert for more than eighteen hours and would probably never forget the experience.

Great excitement and anticipation arose one day at the prospect of a school outing to Aqaba for twenty or so children. This trip was to involve an overnight stay at a small hotel near the beach and none of the children had ever been near to the sea before so were really looking forward to it. Although unable to swim we kitted them all out with some form of swimming costume or shorts which had been donated to the school and packing for the expedition began. We took two vehicles; a VW camper and the trusty Chevrolet. The plan was to drive down the Kings Highway stopping to see the crusader castle at Kerak on the way. This town, almost totally contained within the fortification's walls dated back to the Iron Age. Its precarious and isolated position perched on a towering height overlooking the Dead Sea valley made it a formidable defence; nonetheless the great Arab leader Salah al-Din took it from Renaud de Chatillon in 1136. Our second stop was to be at Petra where we planned to spend the night in caves, sleeping in blankets which we had piled up high on the Chevrolet's roof. This was great fun and I vowed to return on a more peaceful visit to explore the wonders of this Nabatean ruin.

Our arrival on the second day at Aqaba came as a surprise, at least to the hotel manager, due to some mix-up or misunderstanding over bookings but he was sympathetic to the plight of a large group of deaf children who had travelled hundreds of miles and generously allowed us to camp in the hotel car park. In practical terms this meant parking the vans perpendicular to one wall and laying out all the blankets between them. Modesty of a sort was achieved by rigging up a blanket curtain. The mosquitoes were bad that night and none of us could wait to get into the mirror-like sea just a few yards away. I volunteered to lead the advance party while breakfast was being cleared and soon found myself on the sandy beach with a dozen children to whom I gave a strict safety lecture involving a lot of comedic drowning. Thinking this would be sufficient and that they would splash about in the shallows I allowed them all into the water, whereupon every single one of them turned from the shore and started to walk straight out into the ever-deepening water! By the time I realised, the leading boys were well up to their chests and looked set to continue until presumably they could walk no further. They seemed as fearless as wild animals which have never encountered man before – this required desperate measures so I shouted at them as loud as I could. I felt so stupid as not one of the children heard a thing, so scratching around for pebbles in the fine sand I eventually found a small handful and hurled them at the leading children hoping that in seeing the splashes in front they would turn around to investigate the source. I couldn't have asked for a better result as my first two flings caught the leading pair; one on his head and the other square between the shoulder blades. Not quite what I had planned, but probably more effective. No doubt this would be classed as abuse in today's regime, but I was much relieved and soon joined them in the water for a safe game of volley ball.

Occasionally something I encountered on my travels around the country would bring to my attention the more recent political history of the region. Often not as obvious as destroyed railway bridges across the river Yarmouk or the crack through my bedroom wall, but in their way just as formative. An excursion one day to the village of Ajlun provided such an insight. We went to visit two families whose daughters wished to work at the Institute; it being just as important that their parents interviewed the director as he interviewed the applicants. They both lived in this most attractive settlement a 50 mile drive north from Salt through the pine forest of the Debbin National Park in the shadow of its ruined Arab castle of Qalat al Rabadh. Built for Salah al-Din in 1185 and perched on top of the highest mountain in northern Jordan with commanding views over the Jordan Valley as far as Jerusalem and Nablus, it was no less remarkable for having never been captured by the crusaders. That day we had also been invited to have lunch with an American couple, a Dr Lloyd Lovegreen and his wife, whose connection with the Institute was through the daughter of one of the former employees at the Baptist Mission Hospital where he was director. Dr Lovegreen had resided in Ajlun for many years and over a most agreeable lunch our conversation had moved around to the Arab-Israeli security situation, and how even this idyllic location had not escaped being affected in the past. It transpired that in January 1956 the doctor and three other Americans had been rescued by Arab Legion troops when a riotous mob burned down two buildings and started looting the hospital. The Geneva Times for 14th January 1956 reports that violent anti-Western rioting had been erupting in Jordan for nearly a week and that the evacuation of Dr Lovegreen and his colleagues to Amman left only four American citizens on the east bank of the Jordan outside of the capital. Other American sites had also been attacked in Aqaba and Amman by Palestinian Arabs violently opposed to the Baghdad Defence Alliance, the American flag was even torn down in the Jordanian sector of Jerusalem.

The Baghdad Pact of 1955, a defensive organisation for promoting shared political, military and economic goals, was formed between Turkey, Iraq, Pakistan and Iran and was led by Great Britain in an effort to link all those Arab states along the southern boundary of the USSR in a defensive line, and so in theory, protect the Middle East from further communist influence (in effect an extension to NATO). This was the year that Egypt had decided to buy Russian arms from Czechoslovakia and tensions mounted in Israel as Great Britain also supplied Iraq with weapons. America was not a signatory of the Alliance although it did make agreements with the individual countries concerned and thus its citizens were no less of a target for those Arabs who resented western influence upon King Hussein, who along with the Syrian leader, was being encouraged to join the alliance. Ideally Israel should also have been a party, but Arab-Israeli conflicts and Egyptian anti-colonialism made it difficult to form an alliance that included both Israel and Western powers. Ultimately pressure brought on Hussein by the Palestinian activists became too great to overcome and Jordan never joined the Pact. The Soviet reaction to the Baghdad Pact is interesting in that they inevitable saw it as a desire for colonial enslavement of these countries by nations wishing to continue the exploitation of the people of the Middle East and the enrichment of their big monopolies, using the false pretext that this was in the interests of the defence of the countries concerned. Russia's own stated policy in the region was a desire to ensure peace founded on the principles of equality, non-interference and respect for national independence and state sovereignty. They considered that the countries of the Middle East could best ensure their security by not becoming involved in aggressive military blocs. Israel on the other hand, saw the alliance as a severe threat to maintenance of the status quo in the Middle East. Ultimately, the failure of the Baghdad Pact further weakened by the Suez Crisis of the following year, heralded the end of British influence in the region.

11

PYRAMIDS & CAVES

"The mighty pyramids of stone
That wedge-like cleave the desert airs,
When nearer seen and better known,
Are but gigantic flights of stairs."

H.W. Longfellow - The Ladder of St. Augustine, 1850

The idea for a trip to Egypt came in early summer with the unexpected arrival of Isabel and Louise, two Project Trust volunteers from a Project in the Nile delta in Egypt. There they were trying to teach English to three year-olds and at the same time teaching their teachers to speak English whilst re-writing the text books and syllabus - quite a challenge for an experienced teacher, never mind for school leavers like them. It seemed that their school had shut for the summer so their work in Damietta had come to an end early and rather than fly back to England they had chosen to make an excursion. Their original plan to go down to Sudan had been vetoed by the Project Trust directors but being reluctant to stay where they were and not wanting to waste an exciting opportunity for further travel they had elected to visit Israel. Although they had been told that onward travel from there into Jordan would be impossible they nevertheless decided to attempt a crossing of the Allenby Bridge with a view of coming to visit me at Salt. Much to their surprise the Jordanians let them enter, and so one August lunchtime they turned up at the Institute's gates.

I was certainly not going to complain about an unexpected visit from two English volunteers – anyone English was a rarity in Salt, and being female was a bonus! Thus I nobly offered to take a few days overdue leave and show them some of the country's sights. I thought it sensible to also invite John, my fellow volunteer from the Schneller School in Amman in view of the hassle we would undoubtedly experience from a section of the local population who might find the presence of young good-looking foreign women too much of a temptation; a concern proven not unfounded within hours of their arrival in Salt when they attracted a visit from the local constabulary and half the town's population. They seemed to take this in their stride, perhaps because they had become so used to being the centre of attention back in Damietta where causing the odd riot was nothing unusual for the only western women in the port! They certainly attracted attention in Salt despite their modest dress. Perhaps the fact that they were the only two unmarried western women in the town had something to do with it, although this didn't seem to account for why someone chose to take a pot-shot with an air rifle at Louise while she was crossing the school playground. It seemed that a quick tour of some of Jordan's key tourist sites far away from Salt would be a sensible way of avoiding creating any rumours that the Institute had turned into some sort of refuge for single women! How they had put up with this sort of thing for nearly a year back in Egypt I could not imagine.

Very soon all four of us were heading south as we started our hitching towards Amman.   Whilst it was surprisingly straightforward for four people with rucksacks to catch a lift it was still not without its hazards. During one lift, after having squeezed with our rucksacks on our laps into an aged Mercedes whose front passenger seat was already occupied by a policeman - we let John squeeze between him and the driver, I felt the policeman's hand slide past my leg and move on to attempt to grope one of the girls. A sudden bash on the back of his arm from Louise using the frame of her rucksack dealt the miscreant a painful blow and elicited a sheepish grin but seemingly got the message across. Clearly our role as full-time chaperones was not going to be as vital as we had thought – these two were well used to fighting their own battles. By contrast, we picked up one entertaining lift from a well educated Jordanian who turned out not only to know of Brother Andrew at the Institute but also to have drunk beer at my local pub in Suffolk – a consequence of studies at the University of East Anglia. It made a change to fill the long hours on the road with heated debate as to the relative merits of Adnams Ales and Greene King instead of the almost inevitable question "So you're from England! I have a relative living in Manchester; Sheffield; London etc. perhaps you know them?" On one occasion I apparently had an argument with my driver over whether Saddam Hussein, who had just come to power in Iraq, was a good man. I say "apparently" as no English was spoken and I had no idea that I had even expressed an opinion. Nevertheless, I was dumped at the side of the road while the driver sped off throwing some choice curses in my direction.   I would not have known the reason for the unceremonious eviction had it not been for the fact that some months later the same driver picked me up again, but this time took the trouble to explain his actions in English before dumping me once more!

At some point just south of Amman we decided that whilst it was undoubtedly fun travelling as a foursome we might travel more easily if we split into pairs. I was keen to try the slower but more interesting route down the King's Highway and chose this with Louise over the faster but less scenic Desert Highway which the others seemed content to follow. Surprisingly we all arrived in Petra at much the same time just as the sun was starting to disappear behind the red sandstone cliffs. There was an eeriness about our unaccompanied walk through the narrow winding canyon known as *al Siq*, where parts of the three hundred foot deep passage were already heavily in shadow. The heat was still oppressive and I was beginning to wish I had paid one of the local boys for the loan of one of the fine docile horses we encountered at the start of our mile walk down to *al Khazneh*, known as the Treasury. For Isabel and Louise this was their first experience of the ancient city carved out of the red sandstone rock more than two thousand years before; John and I had made previous excursions so had an idea of where we should establish our camp. The village of Petra outside the ruins was a very small settlement with limited facility to cater for overnight accommodation. There was only a twelve-roomed guesthouse and a new even smaller rest house in Wadi Musa. Visitors to Petra would generally arrive by bus from Amman by mid-morning and leave by the same means by mid-afternoon. We had planned to stay for two or three days and I had earmarked a suitable cave (I didn't like to mention that this was in fact a tomb) where we could sleep at no cost and leave our belongings during the day while we explored the extensive ruins and geological formations.

During our short stay we had unrestricted access to the ancient city and rarely encountered another human being, just an occasional Bedouin could be seen tending goats in the distance. Sight of a rare purple chameleon made us all scramble for our cameras, whilst encounters with huge repulsive black millipedes did not! There were also numerous scorpions to be found lurking under the edges of rocks; I even shook a small one out of my sleeping bag one morning (I have kept it to this day pickled in vodka). Less intimidating were the handful of tourists who arrived during our stay, straying no further than the Roman amphitheatre just at the end of *al Siq* and appearing reluctant to dismount from their well-trained horses. The summer sun was blisteringly hot and the sightseers seemed keen to return to the dark shelter of *al Siq* and thence presumably the air-conditioned comfort of their coach. We of course were different. We weren't tourists, we felt that for a short while at least we were explorers living as the locals did in caves, and sleeping under the stars. We'd brought a small supply of food from the village but went out in the early evening following some Bedouin children to their local encampment to barter chewing gum for bread and water from these weather-beaten inhabitants who were somehow eking a living from this dry desolate environment. In this way we spent our three days, and part of the nights, wandering over the rocky terrain exploring all manner of unexplained antiquities and generally absorbing the fantastic and ethereal desert views and sunsets. One night we took a moonlit walk back up to the Treasury and sat inside its disappointingly unadorned but cavernous interior listening to echoing music from a small cassette player that John had brought with him. Sadly, his choice of Chubby Checker's *Let's Twist Again* as suitable ambient music somewhat broke the spell of the occasion as the four of us started to dance.

The lives of Jordan's Bedouin were incredibly harsh when compared with those of the rest of the East Bank population. Whether measured by schooling, healthcare, housing, nutrition, life expectancy or personal wealth, these people compared significantly worse to the Jordanian population as a whole. Although by this time 95% of the Bedouin lived in permanent structures (including 15% who lived in caves) their continuance of a pastoral existence reliant on a land less and less suited through over-grazing and poor management, had ensured their lower living standards. While other areas of the country had improved through investment in infrastructure and to satisfy the higher levels of expectation of a growing population, the *badia* (Bedouin regions) had declined. Parents were reluctant to see their children educated for fear that they would emigrate from their natural community, although increasingly the traditional Bedouin existence was recognised as unsustainable and more and more male members were joining the army or various government departments. I wondered how long before tourists might arrive at Petra and the surrounding area of Wadi Musa and be shepherded around to see the wonderful structures and weathered stone formations including a visit to a "genuine" Bedouin family... At least we had been privileged to meet one and had shared, for a very short time, an experience of the lifestyle they had chosen and which was so fast disappearing.

All too soon we were to leave as the Isabel and Louise were due back in Cairo and I was conscious of so much work to be done back at the school now that the children had gone home for the summer. That night, after a surprisingly easy hitch back up the King's Highway via Shaubak and Kerak, we laid our sleeping bags beside the shore of the Dead Sea and after an obligatory dip in the mirror smooth sea John and I speculated on our chances of making a land trip to Egypt – a country which contrasted greatly with Jordan we were told; a country where Arab met African and where the population of Cairo alone was some six times that of the whole of Jordan. Getting there would be an adventure in itself; we would have to enter the occupied West Bank and travel down through southern Israel and the Gaza Strip before attempting entry at El Arish. I knew that in May of the previous year this small town over 100 miles east of the Suez Canal and specifically mentioned in the Egypt-Israeli Peace Treaty, had been handed back to the Egyptians, and by December the crossing point was open in both directions for residents of Sinai. Assuming we successfully got through we then had to cross the Suez Canal and make our way up into the populous Nile Delta and find Isabel and Louise. The latter part shouldn't be difficult, not after what we'd experienced on their visit to Jordan – it was doubtful there'd be an Arab within 50 miles who had not heard of them! This was the route which they had taken to get to Jordan and so it seemed eminently feasible to undertake it in reverse. Our return journey to Jordan would be much the same in the opposite direction. Apart from being refused entry into Egypt or indeed back into Israel... we couldn't see what was likely to go wrong. There was just the small issue of the ongoing Israeli withdrawal from Sinai and potential local unrest, and of course the fact that as far as we could tell no European had yet made this return journey by land since the Egypt-Israel Peace Treaty had been signed just over a year before. Even the Guardian newspaper's correspondent in a contemporary article I read on my return to England had not managed to complete a Jerusalem – Amman – Cairo – Jerusalem trip without recourse to an air flight from Amman to Cairo.[*]

Even in our secluded location in the Jordan Valley that night, a few feet from the edge of the Dead Sea, we were to be harassed by the local male population. For having laid out our dusty sleeping bags between the rocks on the salty shoreline and settled back to enjoy the spectacle of the night sky with its numerous satellites and shooting stars so clearly visible, we were plagued by a continual visitation from soldiers apparently stumbling across our small group by accident. None acted in any threatening manner, but after a while the interruptions became an annoyance and we made our feelings known. Next morning we wondered whether we might have been visible from one of the watch towers or emplacements which we knew periodically dotted the shore. The starlight had been so bright that we might have been viewed from any one of a number of concealed positions. No doubt our female companions had again provided some local excitement.

Very shortly we became aware of a complication which might well stymie our chances of making our proposed journey to Egypt. As the Isabel and Louise had discovered when they came to leave Jordan via the West Bank, there was the strict requirement that either entry or exit from Jordan must be via one of the international borders or the airport. Jordanian self-respect required a stamp in one's passport at some point in one's

---

[*] Eric Silver – A bridge too far by taxi. Farther still by plane... The Guardian 25th August 1980

journey. Most visitors to the country would obtain this on entry and so a visit across the Allenby Bridge was merely a crossing from one part of the realm to another, and they would leave the way they had arrived. Our visitors had not received any stamp – or perhaps more cynically – contributed to the county's coffers through the purchase of a visa. They were therefore required to leave via Amman or Aqaba with an appropriate exit visa. In practical terms this meant they must take an aeroplane back to Cairo. In financial terms this meant that John and I had to lend them the £120 they needed to do this. Fairly certain that we would eventually receive reimbursement from Project Trust who would not let us remain out of pocket through no fault of our own, we helped our distressed fellow volunteers, not realising the full impact this would have on our own plans in the near future.

It was only a few weeks before I too must return to England and so I commenced my travel preparations almost immediately. I put to the back of my mind the current politics as there was nothing I could do to change them. Gaza was still an issue for the Palestinians. It remained occupied by the Israelis, its western border some 18 miles east of El Arish. The weakness of the first framework agreement made by Sadat and Begin at Camp David was the section on the Palestinians. The plan aimed to set up a "self-governing authority" in both the West Bank and Gaza which would ultimately lead to "final status" talks. Unfortunately the Palestinians had not been a party to this agreement and so the Palestine Liberation Organisation (PLO) purportedly speaking on behalf of the Palestinian people rejected it.[†] In the meantime there was nothing but uncertainty and a feeling of expectancy. There was also the occasional bombing.

Thus was the political background to the situation in in Sinai when in August 1980 we contemplated our overland adventure into Egypt. Ranking somewhat lower down in my list of concerns was the edict from the directors of Project Trust back in Scotland that no volunteer was to leave their host country without permission. Having already made two unauthorised visits to Syria and one to Israel I saw little point in seeking permission to head to Egypt; anyway, there was insufficient time for an exchange of letters and telephoning was not an option as I had known it take five days to secure a line to Europe. The biggest challenge would be

---

[†] Not until 1993 and the Oslo Accords signed by Israel and the PLO was there to be another major advance in Middle East peace negotiations.

to make the return leg of the journey from Egypt - I would face Lavinia and the Major if necessary back in England!

No-one at the British Embassy in Amman had any idea whether a British subject might be allowed to leave Israel via the El Arish crossing and subsequently return the same way. My biggest worry was that while return to Jordan from the occupied West Bank was normally easy enough because passports were not stamped for such a visit - thus providing no evidence of venturing into Israel proper - the existence of an Egyptian entry and exit visa stamped at El Arish (on the far side of Israel) was *prima facie* evidence of such a visit and might have the same impact as acquiring an Israeli visa stamp i.e. a refusal of entry back into Jordan. With this in mind I thought it worthwhile to obtain a letter from the British Consul proving my *bona fides* as a volunteer worker in Jordan – one never knew when an official looking document under a Royal crest might prove handy. A letter from the director of the Holy Land Institute might also be useful. I had also heard that there was now a requirement for any visitor to Israel to have in their possession $250. This was probably a means to try and keep out the free-loading foreign students who were partial to spending their long summer vacations squatting hippy fashion on the country's beaches. I hoped this did not apply to "pilgrims" from the east of Jordan, but there was every chance that given our rucksacks and comparatively long hair we might be mistaken for adventurers. Another reason for anxiety was that both John and I were broke, having lent most of our spare cash to our recent visitors.

An Egyptian visa was going to be required for this trip and this would mean a trip to Amman to the office of the Egyptian Chargé d'Affaires (Jordan had severed diplomatic relations with Egypt in 1979 in protest at the Egypt–Israeli peace agreement and expelled their ambassador). I arrived early one morning in Amman at the correct office expecting to stand a long time queuing. There was indeed a large queue outside the visa section; several hundred Egyptians were massed in the street and being beaten into order by a group of Jordanian policemen each wielding a short length of rubber hose. We certainly didn't fancy joining the queue so made straight for the entrance where to our surprise John and I found ourselves ushered inside like honoured guests. Perhaps it was because we were the only Europeans there, or maybe we looked a little less submissive than the migrant Egyptian workers who had to suffer the indignities being meted out to them if they wanted to get home to see their families. While I waited to see the appropriate official I had the opportunity to study the workings of the visa section from inside the building. There was a very small window quite high up in the wall through which the jostling applicants were proffering their papers to a bored looking official who was sitting at a metal desk below. Each was clutching a bundle of passports, forms, photos and money and was trying to catch the official's eye by frantically waving them in front of his face. The man would not be hurried though; like a well oiled machine he reached up and took the next batch of papers and placed them on the desk in front of him. First he took out the forms and photographs and placed them carefully in a wire basket, and then he slowly counted out the fee before placing this in a large cash box. Taking the passport he diligently scrutinised the applicant's photograph and compared this with their face, though how he could remember which papers went with which arm or face I'm not sure, then he promptly tossed the passport over his shoulder onto the floor. When this pile of passports had grown to a reasonable size a youth would sweep it into the next room using a wide broom. Much relieved that our passports were not to suffer the same fate we were eventually escorted into the office of the Chargé d'Affaires himself. He listened to our travel plans intently and then explained that the border had only been opened for local residents of Sinai six months previously and not even he could give assurance that our travel would be possible – although he was happy enough to take our money in exchange for a visa and helpful in suggesting that we take a ship via Aqaba to Suez. With a promise that our visas would be ready the very next day we stepped back over the mountain of passports and emerged into the baking sunshine; reflecting that some of the other visa applicants outside might have to wait weeks to be reunited with their documents.

On the day of our departure the journey down to the Allenby Bridge was swift and quickly we passed through the Israeli security searches and made our way to the passport control. Here we came unstuck. No amount of pleading and protestation could convince the weasely official that we were not hippies but volunteer workers travelling to the West Bank on a fact-finding mission on behalf of an Institute for the deaf and dumb. Our visas for Egypt and our lack of significant funds convinced him otherwise and orders were given for us to be escorted the few hundred yards back to the bridge. Our escort turned up in an open jeep and comprised two former American GI soldiers sporting crew-cut hairstyles and the long side whiskers of the orthodox Jew. I was not sure which was more incongruous; their drawling American accents or the smiling faces and heavy machine pistols they kept pointing at us. Jumping down from the vehicle at the western end of the bridge we were politely but firmly told to "keep walking". Things had happened so fast that there had hardly been time to take it in. Here I was in a heavily guarded military area where access was only possible on one of the special buses chartered to ferry passengers between the two border posts, walking across a piece of political and military history. How many others had "walked out of Israel"? It seemed a moment to savour and so we paused in the very centre of the old Bailey bridge and languidly smoked a cigarette whilst taking in the unexpected scene in the sweltering humidity and wondering what would happen when we crossed over the bridge's midpoint.

We were immediately arrested by the Jordanian soldiers on the eastern side. They had evidently been watching our approach with interest from their hidden emplacements but as we indignantly explained our predicament a corporal announced that he knew of me and could confirm that I did indeed reside in the Institute in Salt. It transpired that he was the brother of one of the teachers at the school in Salt and so we became instant buddies. Without any further difficulty we were escorted to a nearby taxi and given a lift back up the winding valley road to Salt and a surprised reception.

The next morning we returned early, forewarned and forearmed. The director of the Institute had very kindly lent us sufficient funds in various denominations to be able to show to the Israeli officials that we were legitimate travellers. It was a significant sum to have in currency but we had no way of converting it into safer traveller's cheques. After much shaking of hands with our new-found friends on the Jordanian side of the bridge we again boarded the scheduled bus (the only method of transport allowed to take visitors across the border) for the short hop to the Israeli control. Formalities were briskly concluded and we found ourselves free of officialdom and made our way across the open arrivals hall to the waiting taxi rank. Suddenly a weasely cleaner with a mop and bucket pounced on us crying "How did you get in? Show me your money!" It appeared that the official we had encountered the day before was an undercover policeman employed at the crossing point in various guises. Rather cockily we showed him our wedge of dollars, pounds, Swiss francs and Jordanian dinars and he reluctantly allowed us to proceed.

We planned to stay as short a time as possible in Israel so having changed a minimum amount of currency, enough we judged for the bus fares we'd need given the massive rate of inflation in Israel, we caught a *servees-taxi* up to Jerusalem and made straight for the bus station where we caught the *Egged* bus to Gaza stopping only at Ashkelon to change buses. From Gaza it seemed a taxi ride would be needed to take us on to the border and we quickly found ourselves a willing Palestinian driver prepared to try and reach the crossing before it closed for the day. While John and I sat in the back of the ubiquitous Mercedes, catching up on some sleep and feeling smug that we would be reaching Egypt the same day we departed Jordan, we were suddenly brought down to earth as a speeding military truck, which I thought was just over-taking us, pulled alongside so that the Israeli soldier in the back could swing the barrel of his enormous tripod mounted machine gun round and point it directly into my face! Fortunately our driver took this as a signal to stop and rather unceremoniously our papers were demanded. When we finally moved on he explained that it was most unusual to see European faces travelling through the Gaza Strip - confirming what we already knew. It seemed though that our presence was deemed legitimate and we would not be hindered further. Unfortunately the delay had cost us the chance of making the border crossing that day and so upon our driver's recommendation we alighted just outside the small, later to become infamous, Jewish settlement of Yammit.‡ From here it would be a short hitch to El Arish the next morning and we were assured that the beach would be a good place to sleep the night. The irony did cross my mind... As we approached the sea through fields of pineapples I could see that there were already several people on the beach, sheltering under umbrellas beside a cold-drink seller in front of the dunes. What more could we ask for? It transpired that we had stumbled upon a Jewish family enjoying an afternoon on the beach. The father explained that he was an off-duty policeman and that whilst it would be permissible to sleep in the sand dunes on no account should we stray onto the beach after sunset. At that time each evening the army came and using huge rollers flattened the sand into a smooth surface. In this way they could detect the next morning if there had been any illegal landings or departures. What they would do in such circumstances I decided not to ask, but I certainly didn't want to be near the beach if there was a landing of any kind that night. A pitch on the landward side of a suitably high dune seemed called for. We spent a lazy afternoon chatting with the policeman and his family during which time I discovered that he had spent some of

---

‡ In 1982 Israel chose to completely destroy the town of Yammit, a small coastal settlement very close to the border, in preference to having it occupied by Egyptians but also to allay concerns about the availability of bases for the PLO from which they could launch attacks on Gaza.

his time with the Israeli Defence Force serving in Iran. I found this surprising until he explained that right up until the Iranian Revolution the previous year and the fall of the Shah, Israel viewed Iran as a natural ally as a non-Arab power, they had even supplied it with weapons and provided other logistical support.

In no time at all the next morning we had crossed the border, had our entry visas stamped and changed some money into Egyptian Pounds. The route to Damietta was to be across the Suez Canal at Qantara and thence on to Port Said. I had no idea when sailing through the Canal on the Clan Graham almost a year before that I would find myself standing on its banks watching tankers and freighters such as mine sailing across the desert. I reflected on all that had happened in the intervening twelve months and the exciting places I had visited and the wonderful people I had met. But my year was not yet over; there was still an adventure to be had here right now in this desert land where history was in the making even as I waited my turn to board the scruffy ferry across the great Canal.

Since the Six-Day War in 1967 Israel had occupied the Gaza Strip together with the Sinai Peninsula; land over which Egypt had maintained control since Israel's independence in 1948. In 1973 Egypt regained part of the Sinai when its forces crossed back over the Suez Canal and this desert land thus became divided. Following his election as United States President Jimmy Carter committed himself to working towards a comprehensive Middle East peace settlement based upon United Nations resolution 242 which called for three things: Israel's withdrawal from occupied territories, recognition of and peace with Israel and a solution to the Palestinian refugee problem. Only the Egyptian president Anwar Sadat was amenable to entering talks for he was keen to have Sinai returned and wanted peace if suitable terms could be brokered. He had made a historic visit to Jerusalem in 1977 and so had already taken the initiative. On the Israeli side the new Prime Minister Menachem Begin was prepared to consider the American president's proposals although there was much opposition within the Israeli government. Begin had made a reciprocal visit to Egypt which created an opportunity for the opening of negotiations. Both leaders were invited by Jimmy Carter for talks in the United States at Camp David in Maryland on 5th September 1978. These talks lasted several days and resulted in two agreements.

The first framework laid down the principles for peace and set out a proposal for resolving "the Palestinian problem" while the second dealt with the formulation of a peace treaty between Israel and Egypt. The second framework was easier to take forward as it did not involve any third parties who had not been present at the Camp David discussions e.g. the Palestinians. The two leaders agreed that within three months of the signing the agreement they would sign a Peace Treaty and within nine months of signing that treaty Israel would withdraw its forces, pending full evacuation of Sinai, to an interim position behind a line extending from a point east of the Mediterranean town of El-Arish to Ras Mohammed on the southernmost tip of the peninsula. The Peace Treaty was duly signed on 26th March 1979 and thus commenced the hardest part, the implementation of the terms. Both leaders had agreed that the terms were to be implemented between two and three years after the signing of the treaty. This involved Israel in giving up tangible assets and required acquiescence of Israel's Sinai residents, many of whom believed not in a secular Jewish state but one based on religious right – they were not going to leave willingly. The terms provided for full exercise of Egyptian sovereignty up to the internationally recognised border between Egypt and mandated Palestine, together with withdrawal of Israeli armed forces from the Sinai and the use of Israeli vacated airfields for civilian purposes only. They also required the right of free passage through the Suez Canal for Israeli shipping and the construction of a highway between Sinai and Jordan. There were various detailed stipulations as to what forces Egypt might station in Sinai and what Israel might position on its side of the border, effectively this meant that the Egyptians could not station any military forces in the area. Finally, after the first stage interim withdrawal was complete and Israel had retreated behind the El Arish–Ras Mohammed line, normal relations would be established between the two countries and barriers to the free movement of goods and people would be removed. Of course not everyone in their respective countries or indeed the wider region was of the same mind as Sadat and Begin. Most Arab countries chose to ostracise Egypt rather than follow its lead and they expelled it from the Arab League. The process of implementation took many months. A complicating factor (one of many) was that in moving forward with the first framework, that would create autonomy for the West Bank and Gaza, many parties with vested interests sought to use the Sinai withdrawal as part of their negotiating process. In particular anti-withdrawal groups were set up and new unofficial Israeli settlements were formed. The exact detail of the withdrawal had to be worked out necessitating consideration of what infrastructure to leave behind. There were very real concerns that following the withdrawal renegade settlers would move back into the farms and settlements just vacated by Israel and slow down, if not frustrate, the progress of the withdrawal. Begin was keen to avoid confrontation with the settlers being anxious to demonstrate to his people that his policy was fully supported on the ground. In the end it was mainly argument over correct levels of compensation rather than confrontation between bulldozers and Jewish settlers with which he had to contend. It wasn't all plain sailing for Sadat either, even amongst some of his own people the peace deal was unpopular resulting in the ultimate vote of no confidence - his assassination by extremists in October 1981.

Late in the evening we arrived in Damietta. It was no tourist resort; there was rubbish piled up everywhere and nearly all the buildings made of concrete and clay pots seemed half complete. There was little evidence of any working sewage system judging by the stench and there were people everywhere bustling through the streets dodging yellow and black taxis and all manner of other traffic. As we passed over a bridge I noticed a cow floating down the river with its legs sticking into the air like an up-turned table. I decided to test my theory and asked the nearest shop keeper where I might find the two English volunteers. If someone had made a bet with me I could have been rich for he explained precisely where we should find them and following his directions led us to an unremarkable building where a small plaque displayed the name of their Dutch host we had been told to look out for. There was no sign of anyone and none of the neighbours had seen anyone for days. Having nowhere to stay we climbed through an open window from the building's staircase into a dingy light well and crashed out for the night. The next morning we decided to visit the seaside resort of Ras el Bar, one of the places where the mighty Nile flowed out into the Mediterranean. I felt uncomfortable in this place as the beach we had stumbled upon seemed to be reserved for women and children and although the women were all fully clothed in the water we were clearly a big distraction so beating a hasty retreat we decided to give up on our search for Isabel and Louise and head south for Cairo.

The drive up the delta was through some of the most fertile agricultural land I had seen since I was back home in Suffolk. Palm trees seemed everywhere and the fields were luscious green. We stopped at a roadside coffee shop for refreshment where our taxi driver enjoyed a leisurely smoke on an ornamental brass water pipe. His purchase included a block of twelve small clay bowls each filled with tobacco to each of which he added a small pinch of *hashish* which he took from a leather pouch. The cafe proprietor's young son (he could have been little more than six years old) had the job of lighting each clay from the embers of the last. He seemed to enjoy his work and was apparently oblivious to the impact this was likely to have on his health – never mind his brain! That night we were the guests of one of Brother Andrew's contacts at the British International School. Our host gave us a brief but informative guide to living cheaply in Cairo (a city that was cheap to start with) and then to my delight took us to an establishment where a meal could be had for the equivalent of just 4p. A generous dollop of wholesome green lentils and yogurt was presented with a spoon in a plastic bowl at a trestle table at which we sat on a wooden bench surrounded by dozens of other diners (all male). Each diner had someone standing waiting directly behind him - which I thought somewhat over-attentive and indeed excessive until I realised that they too were diners waiting to take up position on the bench shortly to be vacated. In this way I calculated the business might turnover some five hundred meals an hour – not bad at 4p a plate! If only the washers-up could keep pace; if indeed there were any.

We found a very cheap hotel near in Adly Street for our second night, located adjacent to a synagogue right in the heart of the city; a city which was as busy throughout the night as it was in the daytime. Nothing seemed to stop except for a short period at midday. We became almost nocturnal, resting in the heat of the noon sun and exploring the sights and sounds of the Cairo Museum and the streets in and around the famous Khan el Khalili *souk* in the late afternoon, all the time dodging the nose-to-tail traffic. The traffic policemen who seemed to be sited at nearly every major road intersection provided us with great amusement. Resplendent in their smart blue uniforms and white elbow-length gauntlets they stood prominently on small podiums in precarious positions in the thick of the traffic manically waving their arms around and trying to exert some control over the motorists. One in particular caught my attention outside the *souk* for he seemed particularly ineffectual and comical. I noticed a pattern in that every few minutes he would break off from his point duty and stroll over to the side of the road to have a smoke from a water pipe conveniently placed on the pavement, when he did this the traffic flowed smoothly, but upon his return to his station drivers would start bumping into each other and violently shouting at him causing him to respond with much whistle blowing and more gesticulating. It seemed obvious that he must be indulging in the local *hashish* which was readily available in any one of a number of shops in the *souk*.

On our third day we had planned a visit to see the great pyramids so negotiated what seemed a reasonable rate with one of the taxi drivers parked near the hotel and set off for Giza after the heat of the midday. The journey was one continuous adrenalin rush as we dodged in and out of traffic making our way out to the western suburbs. Suddenly John shouted "It's them!!" Indeed it was. We called the taxi to a halt in time to leap out and shout out to Isabel and Louise "We've found you!" Again I wondered how rich I might be had I the foresight to place a bet. To everyone's astonishment we had bumped into them in a city of six million people. Hauling them into the taxi we carried on in jubilant mood to Giza.

Had the object of my visit been solely to visit the pyramids I would have been disappointed. My expectation of impressive monuments rising out of the desert was shattered when their outline appeared above the many roofs of Giza as our taxi approached. Whether it was the tarmac road which wound between them or the ever encroaching sprawl of the Cairo suburbs which threatened to wash away at their bases like the rising tide of the sea; the wonder of the pyramids was that they hadn't yet been built on! As we walked around the base of the Great Pyramid of Cheops and approached it from the desert side with the sun sinking to the horizon behind us, something of its mystique emerged. The setting sun shone deep orange on the steeply sloping stone flank of the tallest pyramid and the town was obscured by its huge mass. The multitude of tourists being hassled by a seemingly equal number of Egyptian vendors were inaudible on the other side and close to I could not help but be impressed by the effort which must have been involved in the construction of these monuments to the pharaohs.

Isabel and Louise had to head back into Cairo shortly - for we had fortuitously caught them on their last day in Egypt and they were to be at the airport in a few hours time. It seemed that a small celebration would be appropriate, both to mark our meeting up against the odds and to mark the end of an enjoyable and certainly eventful year with Project Trust. A drink in the nearby Mena House hotel was called for, undaunted by the lateness of the hour (it was nearly 2:30 am by this time) we eventually persuaded the night porter to allow us over the threshold. Perched in the lobby of perhaps the most exclusive establishment in Egypt we toasted each other and enjoyed a well-chilled local beer.

The following afternoon John and I returned to the Great Pyramid. I had noticed the signs the day before announcing that it was forbidden to climb on the pyramids and also the stony-faced policeman whose job it was to ensure enforcement, but had wondered whether with the onset of dusk an undetected ascent might be possible. We agreed it was worth a try, particularly as John pointed out that the fine for infringement was apparently only 10 Egyptian pounds. I replied that this was about ten times more than the cost of a ticket to inspect one of the chambers inside the structure which we had declined to do on grounds of economy, but I had to agree that this was probably the only opportunity we would have in our lives to see the world as ancient Egyptians may have done 4,500 years before. On the far corner furthest away from the policemen – who had clearly settled in for an all night vigil, we came across a small group of like-minded Arab youths and quickly followed them as they made their way up the south-west ridge. Although none of the original smooth casing stones remained which made the climb easier, I had not realised that each exposed block was nearly a metre high - this was mountaineering not climbing! Nor had I realised the steepness of the pyramid's face (nearly 52°) and looking straight down our line of ascent I suddenly realised the wisdom of the sign at the base. Still, after about half an hour we were at the top. Judged from ground level the apex of the pyramid was a point some 450 feet above the sand but this was misleading as the top actually comprised a platform about the size of half a badminton court. The views both westwards over the desert and back towards Cairo were arresting with the long shadows of the evening light adding contrast as well as rich colours. Standard postcard pictures tended to be taken looking towards the pyramid complex from the south west as this gave the best impression; it also had the effect of making the Pyramid of Chefren look much the tallest when in fact it was some 30 feet shorter than Cheops and I was able to look down on it from my lofty viewpoint. John and I decided to contemplate this while smoking some of the local *hashish* acquired in the Cairo *souk*. The climb down was memorable for its sheer terror, being accomplished in semi-darkness. Showing great enterprise the apparently nonchalant policeman now stood waiting for us all to clamber off the last block before demanding 10 pounds from each of us – no receipt was offered in return but nor did we receive any admonishment for our blatant disregard of the ancient heritage of the monument. It was then I realised that he was never going to stop us climbing the pyramid – this was his income.

The following morning we decided to head up the Nile to Luxor to visit the Valley of the Kings, some 350 miles to the south. The cheapest and simplest way to travel was by train. At Cairo station, known as Ramses

Station and the terminus for the first railway line to be built on the African continent, we collected our tickets and boarded the evening train – noting with satisfaction on the way that the buffers at the end of the track were manufactured by Ransomes of Ipswich (an anagram of 'on Ramses' perhaps?) I had expected the platform to be crowded as there were few trains, but this one seemed surprisingly unpopular – until we boarded and realised why the platform had been so deserted. It seemed that the savvy long distant travellers had already embarked at Alexandria and there were no longer any seats available. Worse, there was very little floor space either; what there was seemed to be awash with effluent from the insanitary toilet arrangements at the end of each carriage. A small tidal wave washed from side to side as the train rocked along uneven tracks. John and I looked at each other, our noses turned up in disgust, should we climb up into the luggage rack and leave our rucksacks to take their chances on the floor, or stand for nine hours in the stinking tide while the bags travelled in comparative comfort? It didn't take us long to decide, and soon we'd left our bags propped against a partition and clambered up over the seat backs and installed ourselves on the narrow luggage shelves running along the length of the carriage. One of the greasy fans providing a warm breeze whipped within a few inches of my head, which by necessity was bent over and flat against the curved ceiling and the metal bars of the racks creaked under my buttocks as I extended my legs alternately to avoid getting cramp. But I had my personal space – and my sandaled feet were dry, rucksacks could be washed.

As we tumbled out of the train at Luxor station the searing heat hit me. It had been hot in Cairo, but here it was even hotter: 109° at midday. It was still quite early when we checked into the Youth Hostel and surrendered our passports at the reception but the temperature was fast increasing. With a sleepless night behind us it seemed sensible to hit the bunks and get some sleep until the evening when we would go off exploring the town. We had been advised that it was best to set out for the Valley of the Kings at about 4 o'clock in the morning so that we could return before the hottest part of the day. With great relief I laid claim to an upper bunk in a small dormitory already occupied by an assortment of foreign back-packers and instantly fell asleep. Before long I was awaken by an agonising stomach pain which was to prove to be the harbinger of a nasty bout of dysentery which put me into a delirious state for nearly three days. I recall very little about those days save that I swallowed just about every pill we carried in our meagre first-aid kit and that once I had made over forty visits in one hour to the very basic facilities which the hostel advertised as lavatories I decided to move into a cubical semi-permanently. During this time I had continued to wear my money-belt under my shirt for it contained most of our borrowed cash in currency and my own travellers' cheques. We had judged that it would not be wise to entrust this to the hostel management along with our passports and John feared pick-pockets as he spent his days exploring the ruins. By about the third day I had recovered enough to eat some rice and yoghurt and had moved back into the bunk. It was now I discovered that the money-belt around my waist was empty! As I was in no fit state to do anything it fell to John to report to the manager and interrogate the other occupants of our dormitory. I had a vague impression that one of the other back-packers had approached my bunk when I was alone in the dormitory the previous day, but it was no evidence, and anyway I could not recall who it was. There seemed little point in reporting the theft to the police; the theft of cash from a foreigner by another foreigner was not going to be a priority and the chances of it being recovered were remote. In any event I was certainly not fit enough to make it to the police station to make a report. Amazingly the very few travellers cheques I had did turn up. Presumably the thief could not make use of them without my passport, but I like to think he may have taken pity on my predicament.

It was imperative that we now started the return journey as soon as possible. The early morning train back to Cairo seemed the best option as this necessitated walking to the station in the dark and thus offered opportunities for ducking down a side alley when necessary. The train journey back to Cairo seemed swifter than our earlier journey, perhaps because we had seats, and for my part it passed in a feverish haze. That night, back in our old room at the hotel we spent the evening with a motley selection of fellow back-packer guests. Conversation included a mixture of German, Spanish and French with each national offering me their own favoured brand of dysentery remedies. The following morning, well dosed with all manner of tablets, I ventured out to catch the bus back to El Arish more than a little stressed by the prospect of a nine hour journey without scheduled toilet stops. In the event my fears were unfounded, although it was with great relief that I disembarked that evening at the border town.

By the time the bus reached El Arish the border had closed for the day, it seemed I was not going to repeat the swift traverse of the Sinai which had characterised the outbound leg. Given my condition this was probably just as well as a long bus journey was probably the last thing I really needed, but the prospect of a night at the border was not very appealing either. All along the monotonous dusty road from Qantara we had passed endless dunes parallel to our route. Here and there were the rusted out hulks of old Russian tanks, Egyptian relics of the Six Day War, and every few miles the emphatic warning signs ordering us not to stray more than fifty feet from the road. By walking a little way back along the road from the town I could just make out the sun shining on the sea beside an attractive-looking clump of date palm trees. Here was a quiet spot that looked just the place to roll out a sleeping bag and pass a relaxed evening until the border opened again early in the morning. John made a bee-line for the palms; intent on a swim to wash away the day's dust, and I followed with no less urgency – although for different reasons. As the sun dipped below the dunes just visible to our west along the beach I moved a little distance away from our encampment to answer the ever insistent call of nature. I must have been some little time as it was dark when I heard a nearby chink of something metal on stone and thinking that my companion was about to stumble upon me in the dark I called out that I was busy and that he should watch where he was walking. His answering call came not from where I had expected but from further over nearer the beach. As I looked over my shoulder to the shadows where I thought the sound had emanated my gaze was met by the intimidating stare of a man pointing a rifle at me! It's hard to describe the helpless feeling I had with my trousers around my ankles; staring down the barrel of a loaded rifle. Suddenly I discovered that this man was not alone; a camel had appeared from nowhere and there were other rifles pointing at me. At this point John cried out as he too had become the subject of unwanted attention. The man nearest to me indicated that I should stand up. It was not a convenient time but common sense prevailed over more basic urges and I did as he asked. Once our papers had been thoroughly examined by torchlight and the soldiers were clear who we were, we realised that we had been discovered by a small troop of Sinai policemen who were patrolling the beach – we were after all less than half a mile from the Israeli border. They were friendly enough and explained that we were in a military area and must leave forthwith. Happy to oblige, I started to set off back the way we had come only to be halted by the urgent voice of the commander; the area was a minefield and we must follow them along the foreshore to a safe crossing point. For the second time that evening I felt rather weak at the knees.

We were the only westerners to arrive at the crossing point, anxious to make good time across Gaza as I hoped to spend that night in the comparative luxury of the Armenian hostel in Jerusalem. All went well at the Egyptian post and soon we found ourselves in a short queue at the Israeli passport control. John completed the limited formalities without difficult and we both breathed a big sigh of relief as he proceeded on through the turn-style. When it was my turn at the counter I proffered my "Registration of Entry" form to the official on the other side of the counter and stated that I would be passing through Israeli and on into Jordan and specifically asked that my passport not be stamped. Inscrutability seemed to be an essential qualification for all passport officials and this one was no exception. He was taking rather a long time to examine the Jordanian and Syrian visas in my passport but eventually seemed satisfied and made to slide the document back across the counter towards my sweaty outstretched hand. All of a sudden he whipped open the passport at a blank page and brought down a rubber stamp with a resounding whack! What possessed him I had no idea. For a moment I was speechless, then recovering, I explained in fairly blunt terms what impact his childishness would probably have. It was hopeless; he waved me away and was already perusing the next document shoved under the grill. There seemed little point in making any more fuss as there was nothing which could be done – I had an Israeli entry visa in my passport and that was that. Still fuming, I rejoined John and we sat on our rucksacks to have a smoke and contemplate my misfortune. Perhaps it would be possible to stick two pages together with some sugar water, or perhaps smudge the stamp.... Neither option was practical so finally we agreed that we should just brazen it out with the Jordanian officials if they should notice it. Our bus was about to depart and there would be plenty of time to ponder my options whilst we were moving.

The bus station at Ashkelon boasted modern and relatively clean amenities, this was a luxury after the last few days in Egypt and as it was necessary to buy another ticket and change buses for the next stage of the journey to Jerusalem I decided to make the most of them. Our connecting bus was leaving shortly but my preference was to miss it and wait the hour or so for the next. That evening when we arrived at the Jerusalem terminus I heard that a bomb had been detonated outside a petrol filling station on the approach to the city and one of the Egged buses had been hit by shrapnel. Whether it was the Ashkelon bus I had no idea, but that it had happened at about the time when we would have been entering the city had we made the earlier bus caused me to reflect that the day could have been a lot worse.

By the next morning I had formulated a plan for getting back across the border into Jordan. It would involve making sure I was on the last bus of the day across the Allenby Bridge – I wanted the border to be closed so that it would not be possible for the border guards to return me to the West Bank that day. There wasn't much more to the plan save that I would wave my letters from the British Embassy and the Director of the Institute and make a big fuss if it turned out I was being refused entry. Strangely, I was more worried about whether there was a toilet at the checkpoint. We met the Israeli secret policeman again as we exited the Israeli border checkpoint. Helpfully, I thought, he told us he didn't want us to come back into his country. This might have made for an interesting encounter had I been turned back from Jordan a few minutes later. I would certainly have had to tell him that I no longer had sufficient funds to satisfy the entry requirements. Bizarrely hopeful visions of UN helicopters coming to my rescue briefly crossed my mind.

It was the middle of the day and the heat was stifling, this combined with the high humidity and increased air pressure well below sea level made the air heavy and oppressive. There was a large party of loud Americans loading their overweight luggage onto the last bus of the day. They had expected air conditioning and many were showing signs of fatigue and short tempers as the driver and his mate struggled to load their enormous baggage. Here I saw my chance to play this situation to my advantage and made sure that my rucksack was buried in the middle of the bus's luggage compartment under some of the largest and heaviest of the suitcases and then took up my seat near the rear. According to standard procedure we were accompanied by an Israeli soldier until we reached the western end of the bridge and after we had driven across he would be replaced by a Jordanian soldier. This first official had the duty of making an initial check of all passports on the bus and announced his intention with a question: "Has anyone got an Israeli visa in their passport?" This prompted a chorus of voices drawling "Gee, who'd be so stupid?!" At this point my stomach started to churn a little more than usual. As he slowly made his way down the stationary bus it became clear that this was not a cursory inspection and that I was bound to be discovered. John showed his document first and this was swiftly returned. Now came my turn. I knew he would see the offending stamp – it was there glaring out on the page opposite "Observations". Sure enough he asked me what it was and I had to admit that it was technically an Israeli stamp. Despite my protestations that it was not a visa he jumped off the bus and I heard him call to one of his colleagues at the side of the road that I had a stamp from the Israeli crossing point at El Arish. By this time my fellow travellers were really sweating and I was being given alternate sympathetic and irritated looks. Hopping back on again he announced that I was to get off the bus and collect my luggage. I refused point blank. One of the soldiers already had the boot lid open below my window and was presumably looking for something that the sort of person who tries to enter the country with an Israeli stamp would carry... I pointed out loudly for all to hear that my bag was buried in the middle of the bus and that it would be necessary to offload nearly all the bags to reach it. I thought there was going to be a riot on the bus. Suddenly everyone seemed to be shouting at the soldier; cries of "I'll be darned if I'm going to sit around here in this heat waiting while you mess around with the luggage!" and "You're not taking my bag off the bus!" were soon taken up by belligerent tourists. I could almost see the soldier picturing the prospect of two dozen angry Americans in a throng around the bus trying to identify their luggage. Wisely he elected to order the driver to continue to the second checkpoint here I assumed a more senior official could take responsibility. Things were looking better, I felt sure that if I could find an officer I would be able to explain my problem show my official letters and receive a sympathetic hearing. At the next checkpoint my luck continued as I recognised our friend Karouf from our earlier crossing, the one whose sister worked in Salt, and so I greeted him like a long-lost friend. This had the desired effect and the bus was allowed to continue to the third and final checkpoint which was where all would have to disembark, and where there was sure to be an officer. My passport was taken into an office – which I thought was promising and a few minutes later I was asked to follow it. My theory was that if any form was filled in then I must be officially in the country and was not going to be summarily returned across the border – which was of course now closed for the day. The senior official at the control studied my papers (no one was interested in John) and seemed to be impressed with my two carefully worded letters explaining the importance of my voluntary work in his country. So much so that he carefully sealed them with my passport into a large brown envelope and ordered the soldiers outside to take me away for interrogation.

About a quarter of a mile along the road was a complex of small shacks; it was to one of these that I was conveyed. None of the men inside wore uniforms, from which I identified that they must be members of the *mukhabarat,* the secret police, and I was cordially invited to take a seat in front of a large desk and to my delight offered a cup of thick sweet coffee and a Mars bar. My relief at this reception was obvious and it soon became clear that I was going to be allowed to stay in the country. The next half hour was spent discussing the relative merits of English universities – a subject about which I knew little but upon which I was more than happy to profess expertise. Finally my interrogator, slipping into the envelope a document which he had been carefully completing as I spoke, informed me that I was to be handed over to the Immigration Police in Amman and that as there was no official transport available I would have to take a taxi. John met me outside as I emerged accompanied by an armed policeman, and we congratulated each other on achieving our goal of a return trip to Egypt. Soon we would be home, once formalities had been completed in Amman.

John was allowed to accompany us in the taxi – as were several other Jordanians who just wanted a lift. I simply shrugged my shoulders when I discovered that I would be charged everyone's fare, it seemed a small price to pay. After we'd been driving for a few miles one of the vehicle's tyres burst and not altogether unsurprisingly I was ordered out to change the wheel. Apart from my travelling companion, no-one even got out of the car as I jacked it up and fumbled with the spare wheel from the boot – but even this wasn't going to dent my good humour! It was late Monday afternoon when I arrived at the Immigration Police Headquarters in Amman. It was clear nothing more was going to happen that day as the British Embassy was shut and I started to become concerned that I would be detained overnight. However, after a cordial interview with a Colonel Salim, who by coincidence I had met a few weeks previously back at the Institute, I made a promise to return the next day once I had obtained new travel documentation from the British Embassy. Armed with a receipt for my temporarily confiscated passport, I was sent home. Back at the Institute in Salt that evening I nervously explained to Brother Andrew about the theft of the money John and I had been lent to get into Israel, but the expected uncomfortable grilling never came and we made promises to send the money back once we had returned to England in a few days time.

A contact I had made at the British Embassy was shortly to be driving home to England and I had earlier made tentative arrangements to catch a lift with him; such a trip without prior approval from Coll would have almost certainly resulted in my being struck off the Project Trust director's Christmas card list. To my amazement the idea had not been immediately vetoed, but unfortunately my chances of again entering Syria had been scuppered by the Israeli stamp in my passport; for although I had obtained a replacement document from the embassy, the Jordanian authorities had endorsed it to say that my entry visa was contained in my other passport and this would certainly have aroused suspicion on the Syrian side of the border. Nevertheless I was still able to send some of my heavier luggage home by road, including in particular my colourful car licence plate collection and various other souvenirs.

Shortly after arriving home in Suffolk I received a phone call from someone at the Foreign Office saying that they had a "package" for me and would I collect it from them. Arrangements were duly made to meet at Victoria bus station in London. The courier would make himself known to me by wearing a button-hole flower. I could barely take the man seriously when he duly showed up in the cafe at the terminus with my tatty kit bag - the only person wearing a city suit and carrying a black umbrella... and wearing a button-hole. I think he must have been trying to enter into the spirit of the occasion!

12

FURTHER THAN CHELMSFORD

"I did not see the Golden Horn at Constantinople,
nor hear it blown, probably on account of the fog."

W.M. Thackeray - Punch in the East, 1845

W e threw our heavy rucksacks into the back of a beat-up old car whose equally beat-up looking driver had kindly stopped to pick up two fresh-faced teenagers in need of their first lift from a lay-by on the A12 just south of Ipswich. "How far are you going?" the driver enquired. "Bangalore!" was my cheery response. "I'm going as far as Chelmsford, will that do?" (He seemed genuinely concerned). "Fantastic!" Nick and I replied in unison

It was a dull spring morning and we had all day to get to Victoria Bus Station in London and saw the ease with which we landed our first lift as a good omen for our journey. We hadn't planned to hitch-hike all the way to India; the first part of the journey was to be undertaken by bus to Athens, a ride of some seventy hours through France, Italy, Yugoslavia and Greece. Neither of us had a desire to spend much time in Europe and we wanted to get to the Middle East as quickly and cheaply as possible, and as there were no buses to Istanbul, Athens was the next best place.

The bus ride was uncomfortable as was perhaps to be expected for the £30 return fare. It turned out to be an exercise in bladder control, for after a brief coffee stop in Paris in the early morning the bus carried on without halt until arriving at the Mt. Blanc tunnel and the Italian border. We had thought that there might be an opportunity for leg-stretching when the driver swapped over with his mate – but somehow they managed to achieve this feat without dropping out of top gear on the motorway. This did not bode well for the remainder of the journey and so after Trieste and our first proper border control most of the male passengers procured large lemonade bottles for the remainder of the journey. There were a number of women on the bus including a noisy contingent of Rhodesian students who took a more robust view of the problem and seemed confident that they could persuade the drivers to include "comfort breaks" in the next leg of the journey. So after a few cans of rather aptly named *Peevo* beer had been consumed we were on our way again – next stop: the Greek border! We were glad of those lemonade bottles! The girls decided that if the drivers couldn't find the time for toilet breaks then they'd just have to find the time at the end of the ride to hose out the bus – a ploy which eventually won over the driver, though at the cost of his refusing us anymore Pink Floyd on the bus's music system (the only part of the bus which appeared to work perfectly).

It was a great relief to arrive safely and in one piece in Athens. I had studied something of the history of the city at school and felt that a short trip up to the Acropolis would be a worthwhile excursion. There were two other items on our itinerary before we headed north again and continued our journey; the first was to have a last pint of beer, and the second was to secure ourselves student cards. The first was satisfied by a brief visit to "Peter's Fireside Pub" where to my delight I found Tetley's beer on tap. The second required a visit to a small travel agency on Filellinol Street where, upon production of an impressively written letter declaring me to be a student of Dipsosis and Gyromancy together with a suitable passport photograph, I was handed an official looking international student card which I could use to secure student discount wherever possible.

Our brief visit to this ancient city lasted some thirty-six hours and armed with sizable hangovers (as befitted students of Dipsosis and Gyromanacy) we started our hitch northwards; passing through Thebes, Thermopylae, Lamia and Larissa. To save on expense we had chosen not to catch a bus to Istanbul as this would cost £10, and so slept in our sleeping bags under a road bridge on the first night and after a ride through Thesoloniki, Kavala, and Xanthi, in a parked railway goods wagon on the second. To my annoyance there seemed to be no traffic heading into Turkey from Alexandropolis and so we decided to catch a local bus heading east. This ramshackle ancient vehicle was packed full of locals who seemed surprised to see us load our rucksacks onto the roof. It turned out that their surprise was less to do with our unexpected appearance, and more to do with the fact that they were not going anywhere near the Turkish border. Happily someone explained to the driver our intentions and he agreed to make a diversion and drop us off on the edge of the village of Peplos from where we could walk to the border. There was much waving from the bus as we shouldered our bags and headed off down the dusty road to the Greek border control. There were few formalities but we received a great deal of attention, due I think to the fact that there was very little traffic at this time from Greece into Turkey. Finally we were on our way in the blazing sun hiking along an empty viaduct over some very marshy fields. The viaduct followed a long sweep to the right across the swampy channel of the river Evros, a long walk across what was effectively "no man's land".

I had an odd feeling about this place. Apart from the fact that we had seen no-one since leaving the Greek border control, I knew that the Turks were no lovers of the Greeks and I wondered what they would think of two English youths walking in from Greece. Furthermore, there had been a *coup d'état* only a few months previously when the civilian government had been overthrown by General Kenan Evren and the National Security Council, and the country was now under martial law. I knew that the political situation was very tense as the government had been abolished and the constitution suspended. It was the sort of place where one could easily disappear if one offended the military in some way. In fact, thousands of people had been detained or disappeared. It was therefore with some trepidation that we walked past the first gun emplacement in which I could see a shiny round steel-helmeted guard staring back at us. We quickened our pace and were glad to finally come across some low concrete buildings and a huge Turkish flag signifying that somewhere in the previous mile or so we had crossed the border and had now arrived in Turkey. Immediately we were pounced upon by a very unmilitary looking official who welcomed us warmly into his office. He seemed very surprised that we had walked across the border and took some time to understand that we did not have our own vehicle. When finally I managed to explain to him that we were proposing to hitch-hike across his country he threw his hands up in an expression of delight and started to rummage through the already untidy contents of his desk drawer until he found a small rubber stamp with which he endorsed our passports with a flourish. It read *"Otostop"*, which I took to mean that we now had permission to hitch-hike – I had not thought it necessary to obtain such consent but did not want to spoil the man's obvious delight, nor fall foul of any as yet unwritten Turkish law. Having completed all formalities we sat down at the side of the road and waited for the lift that was to take us from Ipsala to Istanbul.

It was now a week since we'd waved goodbye to Ipswich and we had come nearly 1,500 miles. My companion, Nick, had previously travelled no further than Germany and was as excited as I at leaving Europe and entering into a new continent. We had been chatting one day in my local pub in Suffolk after my return from my voluntary work in Jordan and I had talked about making a second journey, this time to India, but calling in on the Deaf School in Jordan *en route*. I had already planned some of the trip – in so far as I'd worked out which visas could not be obtained at the border and needed to be acquired before leaving England. The big hurdle was Saudi Arabia, where visitor visas were not granted at either the border or in London, and it would be necessary to take a chance in Amman. A route through Afghanistan was not possible because of the conflict with the Russians. As a contingency I planned to divert via Israel and Egypt to the African continent and see how far I could make it down to East Africa. My preference was for India as there was a family connection in that my grandfather had lived for a while in Bangalore around the time of the First World War. It was tenuous; but it was all I needed.

As we sat in the shade on the edge of Europe Nick and I congratulated ourselves on how far we had come in such a short time. We had spent next to nothing since leaving home and had now arrived in a country where one could live very cheaply. I had bought a packet of *Birinci* cigarettes for 50 *kurus* which at the current exchange rate worked out at nearly 1/200th of the cost of a pack of cigarettes back at home i.e. about a quarter of a penny. After a couple of puffs however, we both agreed to push the boat out and go for one of the more expensive brands at a penny a pack next time. As no traffic passed us we had plenty of time to enjoy the warmth and flick stones at the lizards. Eventually a rather shabby minibus pulled into the border control and the passengers were told to disembark and unload their luggage. We speculated that this was probably the bus we could have caught had we wanted to spend £10! As it was being reloaded and about to leave, our friend with the rubber stamps called us over and confirmed that the bus was indeed going on to Istanbul and it would probably be our only chance of a lift that day. So with as much nonchalance as we could muster we walked over and handed our rucksacks to the driver's mate to be loaded and climbed on board. It was as easy as that, nobody appeared to notice that we were fresh faces on board so we sat back and enjoyed the ride.

We were dropped off at Taksim Square near to some of the better hotels in the city, but one of the passengers led us down the hill passed the Gallata Tower to an area near the docks where he was planning to stay in a cheap hotel which we agreed would suit us fine. In the morning we set off across the pontoon bridge into Eminönu and up through the bazaar into Sultanah-met to see the famed Blue Mosque and visit the nearby Pudding Shop – an establishment favoured by everyone who had ever hitch-hiked out east on in the sixties and seventies.

The days of the hippy trail to India when all travellers called in at the Pudding Shop to exchange stories or experiences and to offer advice were really past, but it didn't seem right to pass through Istanbul without paying it a visit and drinking a refreshing glass of apple tea; if only to be able to say we had been there. As we exited into the bright light of the square outside to my amazement we were almost run over by a London double-decker bus. This was one of the fleet belonging to Top Deck Travel which at the time was still running a service to Kathmandu in Nepal. Each bus was equipped with a revolving route sign which the driver could operate by a handle from his seat, and which wittily contained some expletives inserted between the likes of "Aldwich" and "Hammersmith". I decided to strike up a conversation with one of the crew to try and gain some intelligence on the situation in Afghanistan, from which I learned that even they would not chance it and that they were obliged to travel down to Jordan from where the passengers would be flown to Pakistan. There apparently they had some buses which they were unable to drive back to London so were available to complete the tour. Nick and I felt superior to these travellers who were clearly taking the easy way out east. I did wonder though whether we might envy them their guaranteed ride and catered-for meals.

We spent the rest of the day wandering around the back streets where quite by chance we encountered a couple of men walking two large brown bears. Each man held a thin chain one end of which was attached to a ring in the bear's nose and the other to a harness around its head. With these chains and the use of a long pole the men were able to control the beasts and make them "dance". Before we could protest their keepers had forced the bears to stand on their hind legs and hold on to the poles. It was apparent that the bears had been taught to respond to the sound of a tambourine and I felt very uncomfortable being the recipient of an exclusive display. The men sought some payment and reluctantly I threw a few *kurus* into the proffered tambourine. Clearly I had not shown sufficient appreciation as the owners muttered under their breath and took the poor animals away. It seemed such a miserable life for such fine animals. Dancing bears were illegal in Turkey but nothing was done to enforce a ban or to ensure the welfare of these wonderful beasts.

After stopping at the harbour near Gallata Bridge to make enquiries about boats crossing the Bosphorus I discovered the delights of a freshly cooked mackerel in a bread roll. Fishermen who had just brought in their catches on small fishing boats were doing a vigorous trade having set up little stoves in their hulls while tied up to the wharf and bobbing madly in the wash from the Bosphorus ferries. This food became a staple during our short stay in the city. Soon we were itching to get back on the road and started to consider plans for the next leg of the journey across Turkey and into Syria where I would be on more familiar ground. The first decision was whether to hitch-hike or see what public transport could offer. I favoured a rail journey; for weren't the Turks fabled for their railway construction? I'd not been too impressed with their road system thus far, so although a fine suspension bridge had been built across the Bosphorus some way to the north of the city about ten years previously, we decided to undertake the next stage of our journey by rail. That evening Nick and I found a small coffee shop near our hotel full of old men enjoying a Turkey v West Germany football match on a badly tuned television set. Here we fell into conversation with a pair of German students who had bravely stopped by and who were also on their first visit to the city. One expressed his interest in travelling with us as far as Damascus if he could obtain a visa from Ankara. I had no objection as having already decided to continue the next stage of the journey by train one extra head would make no difference to our prospects.

The ferry which took us across the Bosphorus to the Asian side formed part of the fascinating infrastructure of this ancient city where the roads were chaotic and we stood an equal chance of being run over by a man in charge of a barrow or an ancient taxi. Everywhere there was hustle and commerce, with street vendors calling out their wares and impatient drivers with heavy hands on horns. The *muezzins* calling from the many mosques evoked a real feeling of a world outside Europe. The ride across the water, though short, was as congested as the streets around the New Mosque. There seemed to be scores of similar ferries criss-crossing between the two continents; each dodging the steady convoy of freighters and tanker ships sailing in and out of the Black Sea. We had a fine view of the Golden Horn and the Topkapi Palace which crowned it, and could clearly count the six minarets of the Blue Mosque which we had visited. There was so much to see in the city, but our budget would not allow entrance fees; food, accommodation and travel were our priorities.

Disembarking, we made our way to Haydarpasha Station. This was the busiest railway terminus in Turkey and the start of the mainline from Istanbul to Ankara. It was also the westernmost terminus of the both the former Baghdad Railway (Istanbul - Konya – Adana - Aleppo – Baghdad) and the former Hejaz Railway (Istanbul – Konya – Adana - Aleppo – Damascus – Amman – Medina) which we hoped to follow. The station itself was an impressive edifice built in 1909 and designed by German architects. The history of both these lines was of interest. The connection to Medina (in what is now Saudi Arabia) was completed first, and it was this line which was famously attacked by Lawrence of Arabia in World War 1. I had already seen the results of some of his exploits where the railway crossed the Yarmouk River on the Syrian-Jordanian border and was not sure whether the line continued unbroken as far as Amman. The Baghdad Railway was started in 1903 and was engineered and mainly funded by Germany which at the time was anxious to complete a line to connect Berlin with Baghdad and the oilfields which it had acquired, and to establish a port in Basra (south of Baghdad on the Persian Gulf) thus giving it an opportunity to by-pass the Suez Canal and gain better access to the eastern parts of its colonial empire. At the same time the Ottomans were keen to maintain their control in Arabia and to expand it further along the Red Sea to Medina. A number of engineering difficulties had to be overcome, not least of which was the passage through the Taurus and Anamus (or Nur) Mountains to connect Adana with Aleppo. An easier route along the coast through Iskenderun would have saved time and cost but the builders wanted to avoid the railway being in range of British naval guns. Passage through the Taurus Mountains required an incredible feat of engineering as the line rose some 4,500 ft and passed through thirty-seven tunnels. Construction came to a halt during World War 1 so Germany was not able to gain the facility it had planned, and in any event Baghdad was then under British control. It was resumed in the 1930s and the final 300 miles section was not completed until 1940.

At the ticket office I was amused to discover that I could obtain a very small discount on the fare to Ankara using my student card purchased in Athens. The first leg of our journey across Turkey was to take us initially to Ankara along the route of the Anatolian Railway, built earlier by the Germans in the 1880s. Comfortable fast trains regularly crossed the high Anatolian plain in thirteen hours. We had chosen an evening departure in order to avoid having to find any overnight accommodation in Ankara – a place in which we had no plans to stay long. On arrival on Sunday morning at the modern capital city our main task was to find the Syrian Embassy from where our German companion hoped to obtain a visa to enter the country. We had forgotten to take into account that the country was a secular state and that the embassy, when we eventually found it, was closed. Undeterred by this setback our companion decided to stay with us and "chance it" at the border - I wasn't hopeful, but saw no reason to dissuade him particularly as he seemed keen to see more of Turkey before returning to his studies in Germany. So, without having seen anything of the city other than a glimpse of the citadel perched high on a hill overlooking the city we returned to the station and purchased our tickets for Adana. Again I flashed my student card; I assumed that as this was a much longer journey I could make a significant saving this time, but as it happened the fare was only 8,000 *kurus* (about 38p) and the ticket seller refused to give any discount! We had stocked up with bread, cheese, peppers and oranges as there was no telling when we might next procure a meal, although I did notice a small buffet car in one of the middle carriages. This train was much older than the one in which we had arrived and comprised separate compartments connected by a long corridor running down one side of the carriage which suited me as it would allow us more space to spread ourselves out and get some sleep for by now it was late evening.

The journey continued throughout the night and by morning we were climbing through the Taurus Mountains due to arrive in Adana at noon. My plan was to eat a meal at the station while we awaited a connecting train to take us over the border and into Aleppo but this had to be revised in haste when I discovered that the train which we were already on was the train that we needed to catch and that we would need to purchase our onward tickets to Aleppo from the station ticket office. The train was scheduled to depart in just a few minutes, and there was no way to see how long the queue at the ticket office was. In the end we agreed that we should leave our rucksacks in the carriage and that only one of us should dismount, in this way should the train leave before I had returned, then Nick would throw my bag out of the carriage door, and if there was time, follow it himself with his own. (There wasn't time to relate the story I had heard from the director of the Deaf Institute in Jordan who had travelled some years previously in Bulgaria and found himself in a similar predicament. His companion at that time had hopped off the train at a station to use the toilet facilities. As the train started to pull out of the station he decided to throw his companion's bag out of the window. Sadly, by this time the platform had run out and the bag fell beside the line. On seeing his friend emerge in a panic onto the platform he had leant out of the compartment window shouting and pointing wildly at the side of the track in order to let him know where to find his bag. Unfortunately, this being Bulgaria, one of the many soldiers at the station took it upon himself to empty the magazine of his gun into the inoffensive luggage thinking no doubt it must be a bomb.) As with many travellers' tales, there was no epilogue to this story. I returned to our carriage with relief having purchased the necessary tickets for the most reasonable sum of 2,250 *kurus* (about 11p) only then discovering that they did not state Aleppo as their destination, but somewhere called Islahiye which I assumed was *en route*.

We had had no time to buy more food in Adana and quickly set off on the unbearably slow journey up towards the Syrian border. By early

evening Nick and I were famished. The train had been alternately stationary or shunting backwards and forwards for what seemed like an
interminable age. We were somewhere in the mountains above the border
and had no idea when we were due at our destination. None of the other
passengers was able to enlighten us and the train's Turkish conductor
spoke no English. Suddenly I remembered the buffet car I had seen in
Ankara, I knew it only served breakfast but I dragged Nick off to explore
what it might have left to offer, leaving our German companion to look
after our bags with a promise that if there was any food to be had we would
bring him some back. The buffet car was somewhere to the rear of us and
so Nick and I headed back down the corridor into the next carriage. After
passing through a couple of carriages we found that the next connecting
door appeared to be locked - never mind I thought - we could exit the
carriage onto the track and climb up into the next one. The train showed
no signs of moving, and we were very hungry.

Our arrival in the buffet car was greeted with surprise by the steward
who seemed rather agitated and appeared to indicate that he could only
serve breakfast. This was fine by us and we soon had a plate of cheese and
olives in front of us with a glass of delicious sweet tea. The train shunted
forward again and our hopes were raised that we were finally on our way,
only to be dashed by an immediate stop and a reverse of direction. We
were finishing our tea when the train started to pick up speed and as we
settled the bill I remarked to Nick "If only we could travel forward at this
speed we'd really be getting somewhere". Whereupon, getting up from the
table we headed back to our carriage and upon opening the interconnecting
door were staggered to see just railway tracks receding up the mountain in
front of us. There were no more carriages for we were in the end car of a
train heading back down the mountain returning to Adana! At this point
we both collapsed in tears of hysterical laughter at the absurdity of what
had happened; a state which ended rather abruptly as we simultaneously
realised the full implications. Only the front four carriages would continue
on to Islahiye, the train had been severed at the buffet car - that was what
all the shunting was about as it waited for an engine to arrive to take the
rear cars and buffet back to Adana. Our rucksacks were on a train going
towards the border with Syria and we were in the middle of nowhere
getting further away from them as the minutes passed. Clearly this called
for decisive action. I cannot remember which of us pulled the emergency
brake cord but pull it we certainly did and as the train screeched to a
sudden halt at the foot of a mountain in what appeared to be a stone desert

the conductor came running. For some reason he had not grasped the hilarity of our situation. I imagined him rehearsing in his head his explanation for the unscheduled stop. Having noticed that we had stopped on a road crossing, and not wishing to debate the matter with the conductor (no doubt there was a punitive fine for improper use of the emergency cord) Nick and I rapidly exited the train.

As chance would have it, in the whole of that empty wilderness there was a car approaching the crossing. It was going to have to stop as the train was blocking its way and as it approached I could see the taxi sign above the windscreen - oh joy - we could use it to take us back up to our train. Undeterred by the presence of a full compliment of fare-paying passengers we proceeded to try and explain our predicament to the puzzled-looking driver who inevitably spoke no English whatsoever. Eventually we must have made him understand, using a mixture of sign language and Arabic, and clambered into the still warm seats without a care for their erstwhile occupants. By this time the train had departed and as we headed off into the sunset in the opposite direction from that which the train had just come I started to feel a little uneasy and pointed determinedly in the direction of the mountain where I believed our section of the train must be waiting. The driver merely muttered "Nix benzene" and pointed at the dashboard; which I took to be a sign that he was low on fuel. Perhaps we were headed to the nearest petrol pump and would then return to join the train – it was by no means certain. Had we made our wishes clear enough? When was the train due to cross the border? I don't think either of us gave a thought to our German companion who was presumably still hungrily awaiting our return from the buffet car. We stopped at a garage after several miles and our driver demanded money. We were suspicious and refused to pay him, signalling that when we were reunited with our bags he would get his fare and more. With a shrug he crashed the gearbox and without having bought any fuel continued in the same direction as before. It was dark by now and we had no idea where we were or where we were headed. As we started to enter a small town I felt some relief as I was confident that we'd find an English speaker here. Halting at what appeared to be a police station our driver indicated we should get out and follow him. There ensued a heated argument with a uniformed official whereupon the policeman indicated that we should pay the driver, who promptly then drove off in apparent disgust.

Islahiye, a prosperous district town at the foot of the Amanus Mountains was founded in the nineteenth century as a centre from which order could be brought to subjugate the local nomadic tribes. Its prosperity was improved when in 1912 it found itself with a station astride the Baghdad Railway. In a geological area prone to volcanoes and earthquakes it also marked a change in climate in the region as the Amanus Mountains to the north west acted as a climatic divide between the damper Mediterranean and the more continental conditions to the east. Apparently the area had been densely occupied in the time of the early Bronze Age and more than forty settlement mounds had been identified - but by now it was very late and we would have had little interest in local geography or archaeology even if this had been pointed out to us; though the town's reputation for being a haven for dealers in contraband (western cigarettes and other goods) smuggled over the nearby Syrian border might well have given us pause for thought.

Beckoned into the policeman's office, which turned out to be in part of the town's station building, we were made to sit in front of an old metal desk in a very sparsely furnished office. I had hoped that this man would understand some English but we were to be unlucky. He did though manage to indicate that we were to surrender our passports to him. After some time, and much animated sign language we managed to make him understand that we had been on a train to Aleppo but had unfortunately been separated from both it and our baggage. In similar fashion he explained that we had fortuitously arrived in Islahiye and the train we spoke about was expected very shortly! Our relief was obviously visible and tea was brought in while the policeman studied our passports like one might study the lyric sheet from the latest Bob Dylan album. Apparently he had never met any English travellers before but after a while we were getting on like old friends. Nick, who knew something of handguns, pointed out that the automatic stuffed into the policeman's waistband was cocked. Assuming perhaps that we were enquiring as to why he did not use his holster, he placed the heavy weapon into his holster whereupon his trousers started to fall down. Then with the aid of sketches on his ink blotter he told us several Turkish policeman jokes. Nick, who had been a serving police officer in England, responded in kind. My contribution was to teach him how to say "What is the difference between a duck?" and to get him to promise faithfully that he would ask the next Englishman he met; whom I promised was sure to respond: "One of its legs is both the same".

Our new friend explained, as far as we could understand, that he and his eleven colleagues had just caught some smugglers from Syria who had been trying to bring *hashish* across the border. It seemed that a haul of some thirteen kilos had been confiscated. Smiling, he then pulled open his desk drawer and showed us a block that looked not unlike a small malt loaf; we assumed that this was the kilo to be used as evidence, although it soon became apparent that this was actually his "share" of the consignment. This was the point at which Nick and I realised that he must have been smoking the stuff all day! It would account for some of the jokes he was trying to illustrate in cartoon fashion on his ink blotter. We were getting on very well in this fashion having offered him a spare packet of king size Rizla papers which we thought might come in handy, and did not notice that it was now getting extremely late in the day. A decision to prompt again for the return of our passports received a positive response and we were treated to an almost ceremonial stamping of our exit visas.

At long last a train crawled up to the platform and we were shown out of the office to meet it. It was just after midnight and our German friend was hanging out of the window shouting a greeting, obviously much relieved as he explained that the train was many hours late because he had raised the alarm when we failed to return from the buffet car and the train guard had instigated a search of the mountainside believing we had been taken by "local bandits", whoever they might be. Apparently the distance from where we had stopped was less than 10 miles but it had taken them some eight hours to complete the journey. Surprisingly, I thought, we were also greeted warmly by the few passengers (mostly Syrians travelling with chickens) who presumably were quite used to this sort of delay. With the tickets for the final stage of the route to Aleppo secured we embarked immediately on the 15 or so miles to the border trying hard not to think that we were quite literally now on the "midnight express". There followed another painful crawl and I could see why so few people used this method of travel between the two countries – and why the fare was so cheap.

As dawn broke, very dishevelled and more than a little hungry again, we finally pulled up beside a donkey tethered to a tin shack which I took to be a railway worker's shelter but which was in fact the border control point. I could immediately see that our companion might have a problem as this did not look like the sort of facility where one could legitimately purchase an entry visa. I was right, and with little ceremony our German friend was ejected from the train by a couple of officious looking soldiers in camouflaged uniform. He seemed sanguine enough as he waved farewell to us from beside the track where he had been directed to await a returning train to take him back to Islahiye. I hadn't the heart to mention that I'd understood one of the border officials to say that the next train was due in two days. Well... at least he did get to see a bit of Syria. There was another delay before we could finally leave the border post as we were quizzed about where we had been for the last twenty-four hours. It seemed that unlike all the other passengers our exit visas had been stamped in Turkey on the previous day, and the train had only a few minutes ago crossed the border. The officials wanted to know what we'd been doing in the border area for so long. Without sufficient proficiency in Arabic to explain about the buffet car I played dumb and fortunately the soldiers didn't persist with their questioning, no doubt thinking they'd have plenty of time to quiz the German, and so let us pass. Aleppo was the terminus of our rail journey, for although the line continued across Syria there were no more passenger trains to take us south. With just a little disappointment we set off to hitch-hike from Aleppo to Damascus, accomplishing the journey in record time and that evening arriving much in need of a shower and a bath at my old favourite, the Grand Hotel. Here we were both treated like long-lost friends by staff and cockroaches alike. The next day's hitching saw us, after sixteen days of travel, safely across the border into Jordan and arriving at the Holy Land Institute for the Deaf in Salt where we planned to stay while we investigated the feasibility of entering Saudi Arabia.

13

CROSSING ARABIA

"...And yonder all before us lie
Deserts of vast eternity."

Andrew Marvell – To His Coy Mistress, 1681

It was the journalist Helga Graham who wrote in her book *Arabian Time Machine* that "Kleenex is a good deal more important in modern Arabia than the camel". Certainly more important it seemed than a wife, judging by the scene of a woman dressed from head to foot in black and squatting together with a hobbled camel in the open back of a Toyota pick-up in the blazing sun just across the border into Saudi Arabia. Inside the cool air-conditioned cab were the driver and his two sons...oh yes, and the ubiquitous box of tissues on the dashboard.

This was our introduction to the Kingdom of Saudi Arabia. Obtaining a visa had been easier than I anticipated, for my visit to the consulate in Amman had been an unusually painless experience. There had been three booths to queue at: "Visitors", "Business" and "Drivers". There was no queue at the first of these; possibly because of a lack of demand for visitors' visas – or it may have been because this booth was not manned - and not wishing to tax my brain too much with the philosophical question of the "chicken and the egg" I had headed straight for the booth with the long snake of drivers attached to it and eventually handed over my papers and received an assurance that upon my return in a few days my visa would be awaiting collection. Indeed it was, and I received my passport resplendent with a colourful Saudi visa and boldly endorsed "transit" and "travel without stopping". I had no idea quite what this meant as it was surely impossible for anyone to traverse this enormous country without stopping, it was probably just a figure of speech.

I should have guessed there would be a problem lurking somewhere; and we found it as soon as we crossed the border. Going through passport control was easy, and the customs search was pretty straightforward too until it came to the point when the officials asked to search our car. Of course we didn't have one (yet) and said as much, explaining that we would happily point out our car as soon as we had found a driver willing to take us across the desert; I didn't think it prudent to add "without stopping". It seemed this was highly irregular as hitch hiking was apparently frowned upon, if not actually illegal. The matter was simply resolved by the confiscation of our passports and our being unceremoniously taken back to the lorry parking area where we might find a truck driver willing to give the two of us a lift. Hunting around for a friendly UK driver was a fascinating experience. Here were lorries from nearly all of the European nations each one waiting to be unloaded and then reloaded in the search for illicit stocks of alcohol. There were even two refrigerated lorries carrying Cadbury's chocolate all the way from Birmingham – I wasn't sure how their loads would fare being dumped on the tarmac for an hour in the blistering May heat while the container was searched. Having only transit visas valid for three days we thought it unwise to take a lift with anyone whose destination was in Saudi itself and so concentrated on seeking a vehicle which like us was also in transit. After coming across a couple of German vehicles without drivers - they had apparently been stoned to death for the crime of smuggling alcohol some months previously - we found a UK lorry which was headed to Qatar and whose driver agreed to take us to Doha, its capital. His vehicle was laden with large-diameter steel pipes which protruded out of the end of the wagon. He was hoping that he would not have to be unloaded to be searched and was anticipating getting away from the border very shortly. Sadly he was wrong, for there were to be no exceptions to the Saudi's stringent search procedures. While we waited, we collected our passports and amused ourselves by chatting with the drivers who all seemed to have horror stories to relate. These were experienced professionals who spent their working lives driving the vast distance between the UK and Jeddah or Riyadh along monotonous and often dangerous roads. The danger came not from robbers and highwaymen but mainly from fatigue or brushes with over-zealous traffic police out to make some extra income through unofficial on-the-spot fines or threats of arrest. Our lorry was a Ford, although all marks declaring this fact had been removed because all Ford vehicles were banned in Saudi Arabia. This didn't seem to have anything to do with the fact that America was one of Israel's great allies, as there was no shortage of other American types on the roads. Other unlikely banned items were Colgate toothpaste and halogen headlamp bulbs. Apparently a Saudi prince had once been dazzled and crashed - perhaps running into the back of a Ford lorry after being dazzled by the reflection of its headlights in the oncoming driver's teeth? In contrast, I did notice some positive things whilst buying water for the journey; I discovered that a gallon of diesel cost only 1/10th of the price of my bottle of water. Our driver told us he habitually refuelled with Saudi diesel just before leaving the country at the start of his return journey to England and that with his enlarged tanks filled for next to nothing he could reach his home town in Yorkshire without refuelling although he chose to top-up in Luxembourg again, where fuel was comparatively cheap, before crossing the Channel.

The lorry cab had not been fitted out for passenger comfort; indeed, quite the opposite. The passenger seat had been removed to make space for a small fridge and a cooking gas bottle; I perched on the latter, using my sleeping bag as a cushion and Nick squatted on the bunk behind. Our driver had no plans to continue through the night and so soon came to a halt after pulling safely off to the side of the road, there being ample choice of suitably flat parking areas!   Setting aside all thought of the "no stopping" part of my visa I was in the process of transferring my sleeping back to the ground beside the trailer when our driver suggested that it would be more comfortable sleeping on top of the trailer's canvas cover. This required some gymnastics to climb up using the protruding pipes as ledges but it was well worth the effort as the canvas of the trailer's roof hung like a hammock between the wooden slats of its supports. The stony desert looked a very long way down from the top of the trailer, an impression exaggerated by the fact that the sand and dust nearest the ground was continuously shifting in the wind which had blown up since the sun had started to drop to the horizon and so the ground wasn't actually visible. Soon we were engulfed in a small dust storm, and thankful that I wasn't lying down in the dirt I pulled my sleeping bag tighter and tried to get to sleep.   Then it started snowing.   This was May, surely it couldn't be snowing? I had no idea whether this was an unusual phenomenon for this time of year or whether we were at a greater elevation than I imagined, but I knew that nights in the desert could be very cold and presumed that despite appearances to the contrary precipitation must occasionally occur in this region. By morning there was just the barest of icing suger-like dusting in sheltered folds in the sand as we rejoined the tarmac for the start of our long drive along the route of the legendary Trans-Arabian Pipeline (Tapline).

This pipeline was in its heyday an important factor in the global petroleum trade. Its thirty-inch diameter black metal tube running on concrete supports just a hundred yards or so from the road was the world's largest oil pipeline system; eventually passing 500,000 barrels of crude oil per day along its original 750 mile route from Qaisumah (near Hafar el Batin) in the east of Saudi Arabia to Sidon on the Mediterranean shore of Lebanon. It helped with the economic development of Lebanon as well as American and Middle Eastern economic relations and it is estimated that piping the oil overland saved some 40% of shipping costs using tankers on the Suez Canal route. Construction began in 1947 under the management of an American company, Bechtel. The originally planned terminus was to be Haifa which already contained a small terminal facility handling Iraqi oil, however, the port was in the British Mandate of Palestine and the conflict between the British Mandate and the Israeli independence movement necessitated a revision to the plan. As Trans-Jordan was also seen as another country to avoid at that time, an extension through Syria seemed the safest and most stable choice. The Syrian route was not without its own difficulties however, as the Israeli invasion of the Golan Heights in 1967 took that section of the pipeline out of Arab control. Argument between Saudi Arabia, Syria and Lebanon over transit fees combined with the advent of the oil super-tanker led to the ultimate closure in 1976 of the section beyond Jordan.[*]

As we motored seemingly endlessly along the Tapline road, its every kilometre marked by painted white numerals steadily counting down from well above one thousand as we headed east (we would be only half way across the Arabian peninsula when the numerals finally reached single digits) I wondered at the construction of this dead-straight road. It was certainly a remarkable engineering feat in itself. Our driver said that the continuous white line down its centre had to be painted by British contractors as no local one could be found who could drive straight enough for long enough to accomplish this task! I wasn't convinced that foreign drivers were significantly better at staying awake than the local Arabs as we thundered past yet another wrecked wagon which had run off the road. I could see why hitch-hikers might be a welcome accessory to any journey along this route - they provided chatter and a distraction from the monotony. I caught myself looking out for the next marker as the only changing landmark visible in this desert scene, and even played a game with myself whereby I would not look at the pipe for several minutes and try and guess what the next number would be. Sadly I got too proficient at this so started counting traffic instead - at least they were painted different colours. Nick was counting trees (he had some romantic notion of date palms and oases). By day two he had yet to score.

The road's original purpose was solely to provide access for the pipeline construction traffic but it soon provided a new overland shortcut for the passage of goods from the Mediterranean to eastern Saudi Arabia as well as Riyadh. The Saudi government quickly saw the potential for this route and the benefits state investment would have on the economic development of the country, so in 1963 it entered into an agreement with the road's constructors for the asphalting of its surface. By 1981 there

---

[*] The remainder of the pipeline connecting Saudi Arabia and Jordan continued in operation until 1990 when the Saudis turned the taps off as a punishment for Jordan's support for Iraq during the First Gulf War. By this time the pipe was nearing obsolescence as most modern long-distance pipelines were then constructed with a much larger diameter and the era of the super-tanker had arrived.

were definitely sections which could have done with some further improvement as my rear perched on the gas bottle could testify! One of the most significant improvements which had been recently completed was a massive elevated interchange at Hafar el Batin where the roads north from Kuwait and south from Riyadh joined. I couldn't see the need for this, a simple crossroads would have sufficed for we saw no other traffic as we approached this junction. Our knowledgeable driver explained that although there was indeed little traffic, a strange phenomenon had been noticed when vehicles approached each other at right angles on the old desert crossing. They became "magnetised", and seemingly attracted to each other, one or other would speed up or slow down so that for some inexplicable reason they would both arrive at the junction at the same time and inevitably collide, hence the expensive fly-over. I had to accept this as a plausible explanation having witnessed a good deal of driving in recent weeks, but I secretly felt that it had been built simply because it could be. There were few junctions on this route, and why not splash out if you had the money? The sight of sodium floodlights and acres of elevated tarmac and concrete was just a fleeting blot on an otherwise natural, but boring landscape.

Passing through this junction on what had now become our second evening "not stopping" in Saudi Arabia we entered the vast area of oil fields around Abqaiq. Here the night sky was permanently orange from the flares of gas being burned off from the oil field (one could easily read a book in the cab without the need for further light). I marvelled at the waste of fuel from what must have been thousands of blazing towers. Presumably it was not worth trying to capture this gas when there was so much oil which could be more easily transported. I imagined that the whole area must have been visible from the *Columbia* space shuttle which had made its maiden voyage just the month before. As we passed just south of Al Hofuf on the approach to Qatar Nick proclaimed that we had just passed a tree, I was convinced he must have been mistaken. Finally, and not without relief, we crossed the Saudi-Qatar border. I had travelled over 1,100 miles sat on a camping Gas bottle; had eaten no meals; stopped only once to sleep; and had seen no trees. I was annoyed about the latter as I would have made our driver stop and pose for a photo beside the only tree in Saudi Arabia - apparently. After grateful farewells we found ourselves again standing in the desert, this time at a junction somewhere south of Doha on the Qatar-U.A.E. road, in need of a new lift.

I knew next to nothing about this country which had gained its independence from Britain only ten years previously. It had once attempted to join a federation with seven other Trucial States as the end of the British Protectorate approached in 1968, but this failed to materialise and along with Bahrain it fell out with its neighbours and remained independent following the creation of the United Arab Emirates (U.A.E.) in 1971. Its wealth was built on the abundant oil of the region, although previously pearls had been Qatar's most valuable export. The land, jutting out 100 miles into the Persian Gulf, was low, barren and sandy, and was nowhere much higher than 300 feet above sea-level. For about five seconds Nick and I wondered if we should spend some time exploring...

It was now five weeks since I had left England and it was still a long way to Bangalore, a delay in Qatar, a country which on the face of it could offer little of interest, would be a needless distraction from the main objective. Before we could change our minds a lorry pulled up and a cheery English face poked out of the window and offered us a lift. This was quite the longest road-vehicle I had ever seen, having two conventional trailers pulled by an enormous American-built tractor unit. Such combinations were apparently common in Australia but this was the first I had seen in Arabia. I watched it perform a U-turn at a fuel station and was amazed to see the rear-most wheels travelling in the opposite direction from the cab. This was to be our lift for the next 400 miles to our next staging point in Sharjah.

By a quirk of history Qatar had no contiguous border with the U.A.E., or to be more precise, it thought it had until 1974 when without its knowledge Saudi Arabia entered into a bi-partite agreement with the U.A.E. over its disputed border which allowed it to retain a portion of Gulf coastline to the east of Qatar. Having already agreed their border with Saudi Arabia the Qataris now found that to reach the U.A.E. by road from Qatar it was necessary to first pass along a 50 mile stretch of coastal highway which was in fact part of Saudi Arabia. There were no Saudi border controls on this stretch of road so for all intents and purposes travellers had to drive across an area of no-man's land between two Gulf States.

As we lumbered along this well-kept road our driver recounted his nightmare experience of a few years before when his lorry had broken down along this very section of road. When he left his stricken vehicle at the roadside and hitched a ride into U.A.E. he had no idea that it would be weeks rather than hours before he would be back again to collect his load. The repairs needed to the lorry's engine could not be carried out at the roadside and so the tractor unit had to be uncoupled from its trailers and then towed to a workshop for extensive repair. The difficulty was that having left Qatar with a full trailer the driver could not then arrive in U.A.E. (nor indeed return to Qatar) without it. Although the nearest garages were just 50 or so miles away in either direction there was no practical way in which the lorry could be taken to them. The only solution was to have the vehicle repaired in Saudi Arabia (which was where it was located) and the only way to do this was to fly from Abu Dhabi in U.A.E. to Riyadh in Saudi from where a hired a recovery truck could drive out to the vehicle and tow the cab back to Riyadh for repair. Once this was done and the truck repaired the poor man had to then drive it back across the desert to reunite it with its trailers. His problems didn't end there though as it was not now just a case of hitching on the load and driving on to U.A.E.; for his documentation showed that he had last arrived in Saudi via Riyadh and so he could not enter U.A.E. (or Qatar) without first leaving Saudi. It was necessary to return to Riyadh and fly back to Abu Dhabi before hitching a ride back to be reunited with his lorry along the coastal road again. All this took over two weeks.

At a roadside cafe outside Dubai we stopped for a meal. Jumping down from the cab I remarked that the driver had left the engine running. He explained that this was normal as he had had difficulty getting it started earlier. For some reason I asked when that was... "Back in February" came the unexpected reply.

Sharjah was to be a key staging post in our journey. The English couple, to whose son's christening I had been invited the previous summer, now lived in a villa overlooking the blue waters of the Persian Gulf. They had kindly offered me a bed for a few days if ever I visited. This was an offer not to be refused and I had written from England telling them I intended to travel overland to see them. It was to be a great help to have a comfortable base from which to plan the next part of the journey. This would entail travel by boat down the Gulf and across to the port of Karachi on the coast of Pakistan, or if this was not possible perhaps travelling overland to Muscat in Oman and onwards by boat from there. However, finding a berth out of Dubai or Sharjah proved to be a big obstacle. The choice seemed to be pay for an expensive commercial ferry or take our chances on a traditional timber dhow. The latter option looked decidedly risky. None of the dhows I could see in the Creek in Dubai looked capable of the journey – being far too overloaded or simply too dilapidated; one even had a Ford Transit van precariously roped to its deck. Whilst I had no doubt that these boats did ply their cargoes to-and-from the Indian sub-continent I did doubt the sanity of catching a ride with one. The ferry seemed to be the best option.

We passed some of the time as we investigated our travel options by swimming in the tepid waters of the Persian Gulf or exploring the nearby *souk* with its ancient wind cooling towers. After dinner in the evenings we would leave the relatively cool electrically air-conditioned comfort of the villa and go out across the road onto the beach for a night-time dip. Here the air temperature and high humidity level brought me out into an intense sweat and by the time I had crossed the intervening 100 yards to the water's edge I was desperate to dive into the bioluminescent waters for a refreshing dip and to experience the eerie glow in the dark Gulf waters. It was therefore a shock to find that the sea felt just as hot if not hotter than the air – almost unbearable in the sticky humidity. The relief only came when I came out of the water when for a moment I actually found myself shivering. As soon as I had dried off I would hurry back to the villa where the cool interior brought on more goose pimples, for about five minutes, by which time all benefit would have worn off and I'd be sitting on the leather sofa again dripping with sweat and thinking about going for another swim.

It was about this time that my companion decided that he had travelled far enough - after all, his previous experience of foreign travel had been a trip only as far as Germany. I think we both began to feel that we were over-staying our welcome with the couple. We had been their guests for nearly a week and had not firmed up yet on our departure method or date. Also, I was starting to feel particularly uncomfortable for as well as arriving without much warning I had brought an unexpected visitor with me. On top of this, my hosts had to deal with a six month-old baby which would have brought its own stresses. It no longer felt right to accept their hospitality and there was little I could do for them by way of showing my appreciation. Also, I could understand why Nick might be content with our achievement thus far. Common courtesy would not let me continue further east and abandon him in Sharjah with strangers, neither would my conscience - as I had given a promise to his mother the night before we left home that we would stick together. So with rather mixed feelings of disappointment at not making it as far as the Indian sub-continent, but excitement that we would be on the move again, we used some of our emergency funds which we'd been holding as a reserve and booked flights back to Amman. There was no prospect of our obtaining further transit visas for Saudi Arabia without a very lengthy delay and no guarantee of success.

As I flew back across the desert over which we had so recently driven, I looked down on the grey brown expanse below and reflected that Ipswich to Sharjah overland in five weeks - that was quite an achievement. All 6,000 miles of it by bus, train and truck - and I still had the summer to look forward to in Jordan. There was more than enough work back at the Institute to keep Nick and me busy for weeks, and I knew we would be genuinely welcome there. By the time we landed I was really looking forward to working again with all my friends back in Salt.

14

HOT SPOT FOR A HOLIDAY

"Palestine is the cement that holds the Arab world together,
or it is the explosive that blows it apart."

Yasser Arafat - Seventh Arab Summit, Rabat, 1974

In June 1981 out of the blue I received in the post a gilt-edged invitation... *"In Celebration of the Anniversary of the Birthday of Her Majesty Queen Elizabeth II..."* The invitation was to a reception at the British Embassy, an opportunity to celebrate the good health of the monarch at the British taxpayer's expense and see if my jeans could be ironed into anything resembling a crease. Somewhat under-dressed in a pressed white shirt and charity shop jacket and feeling conspicuous amongst the smartly turned-out diplomatic community of Amman I enjoyed a couple of hours on the Embassy's lawns in the late afternoon sun - together with more than a couple of glasses of gin and tonic, whilst listening to a lone piper and marvelling at how similar he sounded to the last one I had heard on the Isle of Coll. I had met the British ambassador, Sir Alan Urwick, previously at another diplomatic function and also his wife in her guise as president of the British Ladies of Amman and charitable donor to the deaf school. Great entertainment was to be had chatting to the Chinese ambassador about work with the deaf children and meeting an assortment of interesting people all of whom seem to have heard of the work of the Institute in Salt, but the main topic of conversation that evening seemed to be the recent Israeli air attack on the Iraqi nuclear facility near Baghdad on the 7th June. Israel said it was convinced that this facility was a camouflaged atomic bomb production site which would, in the space of a very few weeks, be operational and capable of manufacturing nuclear material - at which time it would be too late to contemplate such an attack due to the massive radioactive lethal fallout which would be its inevitable result. We did not know whether to be relieved at a disaster averted or scared of a major retaliation by Iraq against Israel which would inevitably take place across Jordan. There were some who thought that it was simply a public relations exercise by Mr Begin to illicit public approval for a more aggressive Israeli stance in Lebanon, and that any adverse consequences were more likely to be felt there. Unfortunately I couldn't see if the French ambassador was exhibiting any signs of embarrassment - for it was his country that had supplied the technology and know-how to build the facility. I simply wondered at how two Israeli fighter jets (just like those which the US Air Force flew over my home near Ipswich) could fly 1,000 miles across Saudi Arabia and Iraq without being detected or shot down. In fact some fourteen planes were involved in the raid, making it even more remarkable.

When it came time to leave we all had to form a line, first shaking hands with the Air Attaché's wife, then the Air Attaché followed by the Consul's wife, then the Consul and the Ambassador's wife and then finally the Ambassador Sir Alan himself. As my turn came to thank the Ambassador's wife she suddenly announced that she had a box of clothes for me to take back to the Institute and left me standing in front of her husband while she disappeared from view. At this point I discovered two important things; firstly, how adept an experienced diplomat can be in making conversation to fit the allotted time and circumstances, and secondly that I was single-handedly responsible for holding up practically the entire diplomatic corps of Amman who were lined up in crocodile fashion behind me all waiting for their turn to express gratitude and depart. In my paranoid state I could feel all the eyes on me and almost hear the muttered "who's that scruffy bloke who can't stop talking to the ambassador?!" At last our lady hostess returned behind an enormous box which I was to take back with me to the school. Before I could stop myself I mentioned that I had no transport, having hitch-hiked to the reception, whereupon she disappeared again to order the embassy driver to give me a lift. At this point, hidden behind a large cardboard box I was no longer able to continue my fascinating discussion with Sir Alan and fortunately staggered away from the line. The next morning at Salt I was up at five o'clock and on the way back to Amman to catch a flight to Beirut, perhaps a little less exuberant than usual, and resolved to exhibit less enthusiasm for royal birthdays in the future - strangely acquiring an indifference which I have maintained ever since.

In 1980 I had wanted to visit the deaf school founded by Father Andeweg in Loueizeh and to which Brother Andrew was a frequent visitor. The small village of Loueizeh was less than five miles east of Beirut on the lower slopes of the Chouf Mountains and potentially within range of heavy weapons fired from the city, but I had hoped to travel with Brother Andrew on one of his frequent journeys by road through Syria; approaching the town from the east and thus avoiding the city itself. The directors of Project Trust had surprisingly sanctioned my travelling there provided I first obtained my parent's permission. This seemed a reasonable restriction, but due to unforeseen circumstances the opportunity never arose during the remainder of my year as a volunteer. However in June 1981 another chance came up and I took the opportunity with two companions to visit *en route* for a short break in Cyprus (the cheapest available flight to that island being with Middle East Airlines who were based in Beirut and where a stop-over of at least a day was necessary). My stay was to be very brief, but time enough to do a little sightseeing whilst hopefully avoiding any bombs, bullets or kidnappings. After all, when was I ever going to get another chance to visit Beirut? The political position in the summer of 1981 was anything but stable but on the ground the situation in Beirut was, I was told, relatively quiet and had been for a little while, although the civil war was continuing mainly in the south of the country. Contemporary reports produced by the Israelis listed the following significant activity around the time of my visit:

12th May – SAM missiles launched against Israeli spy aeroplanes.

16th May – Beirut hit by one bomb from the Syrians every three seconds.

17th May – Nine continuous hours of fighting with 25 killed and 118 wounded

30th June – The ending of a three month major clash between the Arab Deterrent Force (ADF) and Maronite Christians around the town of Zahlah overlooking the Beka'a Valley

Syrian presence was listed as 35,000 troops (up 13,000 from two months before) 6 SAM (Surface to Air Missile) batteries, 350 T62 tanks and 3-5 convoys of reinforcements arriving every day. In June a series of massive attacks was carried out by the Israeli air force on PLO bases in the south and on its headquarters complex in the heart of Beirut. They proved effective and the PLO leader Yasser Arafat called upon the Americans to press Israel to stop. Had I known this was what they meant by "relatively quiet" I might have been a little less *blasé* about my visit.

It is hard to pinpoint the exact start of the war in Lebanon. Outrages and atrocities escalated into massacres and horrors long before anything that could be called a battle had taken place. It could have been a fishing dispute between Muslims and Christians in Sidon which escalated following the involvement of the Lebanese Army, but it is generally considered to have started in 1975 in a small way with the killing of four right wing Phalangists during an attack on their party's leader. That same day it escalated into a retaliatory attack on a bus which resulted in the killing of twenty-seven Palestinians. The next day street fighting erupted across Beirut between the Christian Phalangists and Palestinian militia and the city's population stayed indoors - no-one expected it would be nearly 1990 before the war would officially end.

I knew that the situation in Lebanon was complicated and was very much one of the tragedies of the Middle East. Ever since this small country was created out of what was Greater Syria at the time of the ending of the French Mandate in 1943 it had become a buffer state occupying mountains and fertile shoreline to the north of Palestine and separating Damascus from its nearest coast; thus it was sandwiched between the two powerful states of Israel and Syria. It was a country with a population diverse in religion, politics and ethnicity and destined to be regarded as both a potential threat to these two great powers but also a suitable location for them to carry out hostilities between themselves at the expense of another nation's population; but this is to simplify matters rather too much. A very basic outline of the complexities of the situation from 1975 up to 1982 will serve to set the scene for my visit, and go some way to explain the fascination I had for the area, its people and history.

The Palestinians first arrived in Lebanon after Israel declared itself independent in 1948. This marked the start of the Palestinian diaspora with many thousands of stateless Palestinians crossing the border into Lebanon and finding refuge where earlier peoples similarly denied their homelands, such as the Armenians, had not long before made new homes. They set up their camps in and around Beirut amongst the established Christian, Druze and Shia residents (just a few of Lebanon's seventeen religious communities). There was one thing which made them stand out, and that was the thing which initially united them – their non-acceptance of the Jewish State and their intention to return to the lands in which they had at one time been in the majority and in which they had been denied state-ship by the great Mandate powers. Their population grew following the Israeli conquest of the West Bank in 1967 and the Jordanian civil war, and Beirut became more than just the cultural centre of the Palestinian movement but also, following Arafat's expulsion from Amman in 1971, the centre for their armed struggle. Most did not take Lebanese citizenship but retained their refugee status; not to have done so would have meant giving up their legitimate claims in Palestine. From Lebanon Arafat's Palestine Liberation Organisation (PLO) continued its hostility towards Israel exploiting the weakness of the Lebanese government to create a private army and continuing to fight a foreign nation with whom Lebanon was still technically at war. Ironically, the Palestinians had created a state within a state.

In any conflict there are usually two sides; not in Lebanon - here there were many. Allegiances were made and broken with monotonous regularity. The participating sides often allied with different groups depending on the situation or what was being fought over and new groups frequently emerged. To an outsider it was unclear who was fighting who and what was being fought over. Certainly, to many Lebanese this must have also appeared the case. Fuelling the conflict along with religion and politics, were historical and entrenched positions on land ownership as well as the desire for revenge and simple power play. Added to which was overt interference from Israel, Syria, Iran and non-Lebanese Palestinian groups, not to mention the USA and the United Nations (UN) plus a good sprinkling of covert influences. Thus it is easy to see how the war can have continued for so long.

Early on the two main protagonists were the Lebanese Front (LF) comprising mainly Maronite militias and the Phalange (right wing Christian militia based on the Spanish fascist Falange of the 1930s) and the Lebanese National Movement (LNM) made up of leftist militia and non-mainstream PLO organisations whose leader was a Druze. The Lebanese Army initially kept out of the conflict. The Christian LF laid siege to Palestinian refugee camps in a mainly Muslim quarter of East Beirut which succeeded in bringing the Palestine Liberation Army (PLA) into the fighting. Syrian intervention followed with a constitutional document being drawn up by President Hafez al-Assad. However this failed when the Lebanese Army mutinied and fell apart with dissident Muslim troops being reformed as the Lebanese Arab Army (LAA) and joining with the LNM. Assad wasn't comfortable with either of these two sides winning the war so to keep things going he sent in his own troops against the LNM in May 1976 i.e. on the Christian's side. This political act greatly upset the religious sensibilities of the rest of the Arab world. An Arab League conference held in Riyadh officially ended the Lebanese civil war – though its causes were not addressed. The establishment by the League of the Arab Deterrent Force (ADF) legitimised the Syrian presence in Lebanon as the vast majority of its troops were Syrian soldiers. Meanwhile, Sarkis the Lebanese president (yes, there was a government of sorts) was now without a strong army and so saw the ADF as his saviour and renewed its mandate several times. Relative calm descended on Beirut – though by this time it was city divided down the middle by the "Green Line" separating Muslim west Beirut from the mainly Christian east.

The situation outside of the city was even more complex. By 1977 the government which had initially accepted the role of the ADF had by now cooled off its relations with Syria partly due to Assad's rapprochement with the PLO and his stance over the Egypt-Israel peace negotiations, and so it began the task of rebuilding the Lebanese Army.

President Assad maintained a large presence in Lebanon but despite this his forces did not occupy the south of the country which crucially was controlled with Israeli backing by Christian militias led by former Lebanese Army officers.   South Lebanon now became the critical area where all parties had an interest. Israel wanted to ensure that there was no Muslim or Palestinian presence near its border while Syria wanted to reduce Israeli control and thus their threat to its national security; the Lebanese government wanted to regain control in order to build on the relative peace in the capital while the Christian militias most definitely wanted to keep it for themselves, feeling threatened by the PLO - who in turn wanted control of the area in order to afford themselves greater freedom away from the writ of the ADF. The fighting which resulted led to mass migration of the indigenous Shia Muslim and Maronite Christian population, hastened in 1978 by the Israeli Defence Force (IDF) troops who moved north across the border in response to PLO attacks upon Tel Aviv.   By mid-1978 United Nations resolution 425 called for Israeli withdrawal and UN troops came in to replace the Israelis.   Largely impotent, the UN was unable to do more than observe the fighting and the void left by the Israelis was taken up by Haddad's South Lebanese Army (SLA), previously the Free Lebanese Army.

By 1980 the Shias had grown in importance leading to fighting in the south between Shia *Amal* and the PLO in the guise of *Fatah.* By the time of my visit in the summer of 1981 there was an Israeli-Palestinian ceasefire in the south which had been brokered by Philip Habib, the envoy of the US President Reagan.   This was of course only a truce between two of the warring parties and the Phalangist militia continued to grow. By this time the people of Beirut were starting to see that the extremists could not bring order and a moderate middle was beginning to grow in importance.[*] Ignorant of the nuances of the various disputes I arrived at the airport terminal in West Beirut and immediately thought: "What on earth have I

---

[*] By 1982 Phalangists had become a serious threat to Arafat's PLO and Assad's ADF. In June of that year Israel had invaded Lebanon and the Israeli Defence Force (IDF) had encircled and was launching attacks on Beirut. Ostensibly this was in reaction to an assassination attempt upon Israel's ambassador to London. By August American, French and Italian troops had arrived in the city to oversee the departure of Arafat and his PLO. Again a void was created which the Israelis were quick to fill by occupying West Beirut. Shortly after there were the terrible massacres in the Sabra and Chatila camps so recently vacated by the PLO fighters, many of whom had left their families behind. There followed more murders, bombings, kidnappings and presidential assassinations together with campaigns of terror against foreign diplomats, then in 1983 came the arrival of a small British contingent and the bombing of the American embassy which would ultimately lead to the USA withdrawing its troops the following year.

stepped into?" The place was a complete mess. There were piles of rubble lying around the arrivals hall and ceiling tiles hanging down looking like they would any minute fall on someone's head, but most alarming were the lines of bullet holes tracking across the walls and whole chunks missing from the building. I noticed by way of contrast the immaculate creases in the short-sleeved shirt worn by the immigration officer who for some reason was trying to tell me that I was not going to be allowed into the country because of an irregularity with my visa. How could this be? Here was a country into which military tanks could be brought and any amount of goods and weapons smuggled and I was not going to be allowed to visit! It seemed that an over-enthusiastic Greek official had stamped his country's entry and exit stamps on the same page as my Lebanese visa and these having smudged looked rather similar to Lebanese stamps. It was either my scruffy appearance indicating I was someone who was unlikely to have surplus funds to pay a *baksheesh,* or it was the fact that I was accompanied by a man in clerical attire and the official was himself a Christian, that led him to finally shrug his shoulders and let me through. Out front in the humid heat was a line of taxis looking like a beauty parade at a scrap yard. We piled into the first of these and headed east, skirting around the city and up into the hills.

Our stay at the Deaf School, located in a former villa and night club overlooking the sprawling city below, was to be brief. Early the next morning we piled into the school's VW minibus and headed down into Beirut to pick up the coast road north. A few yards down the road we encountered a group of tanks, Syrian apparently, well dug in, and all with their muzzles pointing in the direction of the centre of Beirut. They had clearly been there sometime and looked intent on staying. At nearly every junction there seemed to be check-points where we were challenged and asked for our documents by an assortment of young men, sometimes uniformed and sometimes not, but all excessively well armed, except for the Lebanese police - rather ironic I thought.

Our route down into the city would inevitably take us across the Green Line. This was a no-man's land between the Muslim and Christian areas snaking up through the city and in places enclosing office blocks, apartments and formally luxury hotels. Grass grew out of the mud and dust of the streets and mature trees sprouted from within buildings. Everywhere there were signs of the intense fighting which had taken place not long before. Piles of battered oil drums, peeling signs, lamp posts bent into impossible shapes. Every building was pock-marked from the impact of shells, mortars and bullets and most windows had been enlarged into gaping orifices indicating that at some point there had been fighters in that position whom their opponents had sought to dislodge with what appeared to be excessive force. This was not what I had expected; it seemed more reminiscent of some of the old black and white images of towns devastated by the massed armies which had criss-crossed Europe forty years before. It was hard to believe that this was the result of enthusiastic and often teenage amateur fighters using some of the most sophisticated weapons available. I had met one such fighter called "Bardo"; he was an Armenian youth and had been taken in for a time under the wing of Father Andeweg at the deaf school and accompanied him once on a visit to Salt. His appearance was not that dissimilar to my own: tall, thin and rather shaggy looking, but there the resemblance ended. He had been orphaned quite young and had grown up on the anarchic streets of Beirut where he had many times travelled around on the back of a friend's motorbike brandishing, and by his own account firing, his Kalashnikov. He seemed quite unsettled, perhaps unsurprisingly, and I often wondered what became of him subsequently.

There were a number of further checkpoints to pass before our driver, Brother Andrew, put his foot to the floor and sped (in so far as it's possible in a VW camper van) over the main crossing in the company of a convoy of other drivers. It seemed that this was not a place to be caught hanging around as snipers still occasionally operated. Brother Andrew recounted the tale of his going to collect a volunteer from the airport one day. Once loaded with the volunteer and all his gear for a year's stay they were hijacked by a group of armed men who demanded at gunpoint that they hand over the minibus. This they duly did and were left shaken but safe by the side of the road. The poor volunteer had been in the country for less than an hour and had lost everything – except his life. Oddly, some months later Brother Andrew came across the same minibus in use by a group of militia and amazingly was able to persuade the group's leader to return it to the school complete with camouflage paint and a turret hole cut through its roof for a machine gun mounting! On another occasion whilst heading east across the Green Line the clutch had failed in the van in which he was travelling and he had been forced to get out and push. He could only assume that he avoided getting shot at as every sniper in the vicinity was probably rolling around in stitches laughing at the absurd sight of a cleric pushing a minibus along a road in one of the most dangerous places in the world at that time, while other traffic sped by at top speed. Luckily, on this occasion we crossed safely.

I had experienced the traffic of Cairo and Istanbul and thought I had seen all possible manoeuvres but the drive north out of the city took this experience to a new level. The coast road on the edge of the city was in part a splendid six lane carriageway with three carriageways in both directions, in this section there happened to be one junction with a dual carriage way where traffic crossing at right angles was completely uncontrolled. Traffic was uncontrolled everywhere of course, there being little point in obeying laws which no one could enforce - especially if they weren't going to pay taxes or traffic policemen (or even traffic light maintenance crews). In order to cross this busy interchange, blocked by the crossing traffic, the vehicles going north simply used up all six carriageways. Unfortunately the vehicles heading south had the same idea. The ensuing chaos would have been amusing to watch had I not been sat in a cramped van in 90°F heat with only limited time in which to see something of the country. Ultimately we arrived at the ancient port of Tripoli and after taking a few photographs I sat in a street-side coffee shop enjoying a black market American-brand cigarette and a cup of thick Turkish coffee while gazing over the harbour and wondered at the number of scruffy freighters all lined up waiting to deliver their cargoes of guns and other western produce. Meanwhile, back in Beirut, the Israeli air force had dropped a massive bomb somewhere on the city.

Arrival at Larnaca Airport in Cyprus was a relief. There were no guns visible and all the doors seemed to be still hanging from their hinges. Here we parted company with Brother Andrew, arranging to meet back at the airport in a few days time. Our plan was to head west to Limassol where we hoped to be able to find a floor to sleep on in a church hall somewhere and then head up into the Troudos Mountains dominated by the 6,400 feet Mount Olympus. We had no difficulty in finding a suitable place to sleep out in the woods surrounding the mountain after a long day on the local transport, a former *alpenbus,* winding up the hairpin road into the mountains. At one point in order to negotiate a particularly tight bend it reversed, and due to the unusually long overhang behind the rear axle I found myself with other passengers on the rear seats hanging well out over a sheer precipice. Not for the first time memories of the film "The Italian Job" sprang to mind, and also flashback images of the two wrecks we had passed in the gorges during our ascent.

All too soon it was time to think about returning to Jordan, but first I thought it worth paying a visit to Nicosia, another divided city - this time divided between the Turks and the Greek Cypriots. I walked along the southern edge of this city's "Green Line" or buffer zone. This time the decay visible as one peered across from official viewpoints was as a result of abandonment rather than battle. The buildings were on the whole intact, but the appearance of seven years of neglect was accentuated by the contrast with the newer and thriving relocated shopping streets just to the south. We stayed briefly in the flat of someone whom I recall owned a couple of restaurants on opposite sides of the world; I guess Cyprus was about the mid-point for commuting. They kindly offered us their living room floor for the night before we made our way back down to the airport and I found myself again on a flight heading into Beirut. This time we were to transit at the airport, merely stopping long enough to change planes. While we waited in the transit lounge we learned that the airport had been closed earlier that morning as there had been shooting across the runway. Obviously I was delighted that the situation had improved enough for them to consider it safe for us to land, but I was beginning to learn that "safe" was also a relative concept in this country. We also had to take off again of course, and unsurprisingly perhaps, departure was delayed several hours while we waited; either for more bullets, or the absence of bullets, it was never made clear. As the plane's wheels finally left the ground I imagined it rising faster as the passengers all collectively exhaled.

15

HOMEWARD BOUND

I hear a voice you cannot hear,
Which says, I must not stay;
I see a hand you cannot see,
Which beckons me away.

Thomas Tickell - Colin and Lucy, 1725

On that sunny day in July when Prince Charles and Lady Diana Spencer were exchanging their wedding vows at St Paul's Cathedral Nick and I were busy helping to demolish one wing of the Institute which had been used to house the old people's home. We were using an enormous jack-hammer linked to an over-sized compressor which had been loaned to the school by a British construction company carrying out extension works at Amman airport. Also hard at work was Mike, the new Project Trust volunteer who had taken over from me the previous autumn. The idea was to retain the lower ground floor structure but demolish the remainder, most of which had already been knocked down rather carelessly by a local contractor with his own JCB digger. We were primarily needed to tidy up the rubble and convert the remaining structure into a cistern. The school was desperately in need of new water storage facilities as one of the two existing underground tanks was leaking and had been filled in. The plan was quite simple and involved concreting up doorways and windows and cutting a hatchway through from above. We had already installed the plumbing and would shortly hand the structure over to some local builders who would coat the interior with waterproof render. Mike was half listening to the wedding service on a crackling shortwave radio in between bursts of noisy drilling. For me it all seemed so remote and I was only partly looking forward to returning to England to take up my place at Polytechnic. Of course there was still the adventure of the return journey. It had taken sixteen days to travel here and I hoped to return in fourteen, leaving a full month to continue helping Mike at the Institute with the myriad of jobs which needed completing before the children returned to school in September.

A little earlier I had travelled down with some of the children to the Allenby Bridge on the UNRWA bus at the start of their journey home to their villages and camps in West Bank and Gaza. Most of the children went home this way although a few were collected by parents or uncles and aunts living on the east bank of the Jordan. The bus drove straight to the eastern end of the bridge where formalities commenced. Dismounting as requested, I walked with one of the teachers accompanied by two Jordanian soldiers, one an officer and the other as far as I could tell a private. We also had an UNRWA representative who would accompany the children across the bridge and onward on their journey. In what seemed a comic charade the United Nations official handed some papers to the Jordanian officer who in turn handed them to his soldier. He in turn passed them on to an Israeli soldier who had joined the small group a few yards from me standing near the centre of the bridge. Without a glance at them he also passed them to his officer who then asked him a question. This in turn was relayed back down the chain and across and up the other side. This process continued like a children's game of pass the parcel until the two officers, standing only three feet apart, were satisfied that all was in order. It was clear that everyone understood and spoke Arabic, Hebrew as well I suspected, but the requirement for non-fraternisation was preserved by this pretence and the business of the United Nations was effectively concluded. Back at the Institute the lads had packed up for the day and arrangements had been made for the builders to come the next morning to render the cistern's internal walls. That evening under sufferance I put aside my reservations on royal celebrations as we toasted the royal couple with a couple of bottles of locally brewed Amstel beer then went late to bed.

Sometime in the middle of the night I was woken by Joshua who had in turn been woken by the sound of continuous rushing noise coming from outside his apartment. He had quickly realised that it was the sound of water rushing out of the pipe supplying the new cistern and echoing around the vacant structure. We had completed the plumbing but forgotten to close the taps and now the weekly water supply was arriving and filling the tank before it had been made waterproof. It wasn't just the waste of water which concerned him but the fact that if the structure was too wet the builders would not work and would go away probably never to be seen again that month. I awoke Nick and we soon discovered that the situation was critical; the building was already nearly two feet deep in water. Hundreds of gallons must have been pumping in for hours! Armed with as many buckets as we could find Nick and I dropped down into the black interior and filled them as fast as we could while Mike stayed up top hauling them up and tipping them out over the bank. After a while a small army of helpers assembled and Joshua brought a light so that we were no longer working in complete darkness. Slowly the water level dropped as bucket after bucket was emptied. We changed roles regularly to give our arms a rest but still it was nearly breakfast before we had the last drop of water away. I'm not sure who it was who blamed the Prince and Princess for our exhausting night; perhaps if they hadn't got married we might not have drunk the beer and might not have slept so soundly; not for the first time I resolved to ignore any future royal celebrations.

We completed many jobs that month; and started several more. Mike had spent a whole year working flat out as I had done previously and he too was shortly to have to leave Salt for good and might never have another opportunity for exploring. Apart from our short trip to Beirut and Cyprus Mike had hardly taken any leave so we felt it would be a good opportunity if he were to accompany us into Syria when we left. We were all keen to see the ancient caravan oasis at Palmyra out in the Syrian Desert which had only the previous year been recommended for inclusion as a UNESCO world heritage site. I had visited there once before and had been captivated by its remoteness and the huge extent of the ancient ruins. Unlike Jerash in Jordan, there were no tourists and no accommodation had been made to cater for visitors so I could virtually guarantee that we would have the entire site to ourselves.

Farewells were made as I again wished Brother Andrew and all his helpers the very best fortune. This time I felt that I was leaving for good, as I was about to embark on a further period of education when I returned to England and had no idea what would follow and whether there would be another opportunity to return.

A *servees-taxi* took the three of us to Damascus where we were again greeted warmly as cherished customers by our now old friends at the Grand Hotel. There had been a recent car bomb explosion in the city but we detected no signs of unrest as we spent the evening wandering in the *souk*. An early morning start in a second taxi took us the 100 miles north to Homs from where we were forced to hitch-hike the remaining 90 miles of rough road through the desert to Palmyra. We bailed out of our pickup truck at the edge of the oasis just before entering the small town known in Arabic as Tadmor. Here small sandy stone-walled paths weaved between sunken plots of orange trees whose grass covered bases, to my surprise, were some six to ten feet lower than the paths. The continual irrigation over centuries of these small shady plots had caused their level to sink while the bone dry pathways remained like galleries looking down upon then. This we discovered just in time before Mike vaulted over a low wall having spied what he thought to be a suitable site for us to lay out our sleeping bags and make camp beneath an especially shady orange tree. We left our kit here and after a quick snack set out to cover the 2 miles or so through the ruins towards the distant hill top castle of Qalaat Shirkuh. The castle post-dated the ruins by many centuries but its splendid position atop a solitary hill to the west of the ancient city made it a superb viewpoint from which to gaze in awe at what had earlier been a settlement at the centre of an empire.

Palmyra contained the ruins of a great city once one of the most important cultural centres of the ancient world and the site itself had been occupied since Palaeolithic and Neolithic eras. Dominated by the Great Temple of Bel, its monuments dating back to the first and second centuries married Graeco-Roman techniques with Persian influences. We followed the grand colonnaded street for more than half a mile walking past numerous temples and beyond the surrounding walls over the remains of the Roman aqueduct and through desert dotted with multi-roomed stone funerary towers. These were seemingly placed at random and formed part of an immense necropolis comprising tombs for the rich of the city. The climb up to the castle was steep and exhausting in the oppressive heat especially after a long trek across from the oasis, but the view from the top was worth it - once we'd figured out how to get into the castle for there was a deep moat carved into the rock which had not been visible from below. There was no longer a bridge over the moat, though its pillars remained, and we had to climb some 30 feet down and up the other side to gain entry. Although ruined, this castle contained a labyrinth of different levels and was a treasure which very few modern-day tourists had visited. Palmyra reached great prominence in Roman times when it formed part of a caravan route linking the Roman Empire with Persia, India and China. Like Petra and Jerash in Jordan it was one of the three great cities of the classical period in the Middle East owing its prosperity and indeed existence as a city to ancient trade routes.

Next morning after a pleasant night listening to cicadas and the distant bleating of goats we walked into the centre of the little town from where we hoped we might more easily catch a lift back to Homs. Situated roughly midway between Damascus and the river Euphrates on the northern side of a small oasis, Tadmor supported a population of about 18,000 inhabitants. Unremarkable save for its notorious prison (a former French Mandate fort and now a place of incarceration for the regime's political opponents) and a military fighter base to the north east, this little town squatting in more than 100°F of sweltering heat was mercifully hidden from the view of Palmyra's ruins by the ancient oasis in which we had made our camp.

It was at this prison on 27th June 1980 that Rifaat al-Assad took revenge for a failed assassination attempt upon his brother President Hafez al-Assad the previous day during a reception for the president of Mali. A grenade had landed at the president's feet following a burst of machine gun fire, thrown by a disaffected supporter of the Islamist group the Muslim

Brotherhood. Syrian soldiers under Rifaat's command were dispatched to the prison which housed hundreds of members and supporters of the Muslim Brotherhood with orders to execute them in their cells. Records were not kept of prisoners held at the prison so no-one can be sure of the numbers killed, but estimates ranged from 500 to over 2,000. My previous visit to Palmyra had been only a few days before the massacre. Details of the tragedy did not emerge until much later, and had I been aware of them as we sat in our shady grove after an afternoon's exploring and enjoying a wonderful view of the ruins silhouetted by the setting sun I'm sure much of the beauty and antiquity around us would have seemed less appealing.

I had known the previous summer of the disturbances in Syria. President Hafez al-Assad was embroiled in one of the biggest crises of his presidency; a full-scale uprising by the Muslim Brotherhood, an organisation for which membership had just been made a capital offence. This Islamist group, nominally a branch of the group founded in 1920s Egypt was first banned in Syria in 1958 during the time of the United Arab Republic (UAR) when Syria merged with Egypt under President Nasser partly as an expedient to counter the communist threat to the country. The Brotherhood opposed the nationalist regime of the Ba'ath Party and returned to politics in 1961 after the dissolution of the UAR. Banned again after the 1963 Ba'athist coup, the now underground movement with its power base amongst the Sunni Muslims of Hama and Aleppo took against the ruling minority Alawite sect - brought into ascendency after the accession of Hafez al-Assad (himself an Alawite) to the presidency in 1970. For ten years they had conducted sporadic violence against Assad's regime and in 1979 were implicated in the murder of a group of Alawite army cadets following a targeted assassination campaign. The assassination attempt upon the president in 1980 was taken as justification for a policy of retribution against the Muslim Brotherhood.

During my visit to Syria the previous June I had been warned against travel north to Aleppo as the city was closed due to fighting between Assad's forces and supporters of the Muslim Brotherhood. I was told that the city of Hama was also closed for the same reason, but I was keen to see for myself the great wooden water wheels on the Orontes which flowed through the town. Here was the largest collection of water wheels, or norias, in the world. They were pictured on the national bank notes and to not see them while I was in the country would be like going to England and not seeing Stonehenge. There were still seventeen of them dating back to the twelfth and thirteenth centuries, the largest of which was the al-Mohamadiya, some 66 feet in diameter. Aqueducts and other channels were also built to take water lifted from the Orontes to use for irrigation of nearby fields. I had left my friendly lorry driver who had given me a lift up from Homs and flagged down a local taxi which seemed to be heading down into the town. Its driver, a Christian, was reluctant at first to take me, he explained that there had just been shooting between the army and the Brotherhood at the station and the town was not safe. It was certainly not safe for a foreigner to walk around and I agreed to remain in his car if he would drive me to one or two of the main sites. When we arrived at the large noria the scene looked normal enough; there were children playing on the banks of the river and I could hear their cries above the sound of the creaking of its ancient timbers as the enormous wheel was rotated by the river's flow. A number of people were walking by and I judged it safe enough to get out of the car to take a photo. Just as I was climbing back in I heard gunfire and suddenly everyone in view was running. With no idea of the location of the gunman I fell into the back seat of the taxi and we sped off. With thumping heart I thanked my driver and asked to be taken back up to the roundabout - a journey he was more than happy to make. He would accept no fare and even apologised for the distress his fellow countrymen may have caused me. I had no inkling then that within a year I would be back in Syria where little would have changed on the political map; those isolated shootings turned out to be part of a series of attacks which took place in Hama in 1980 and 1981.

Just a few months earlier, as Nick and I had been passing through Syria on the out-bound leg of our journey in April of 1981, government forces killed hundreds in the city in response to a hit-and-run attack on a nearby Alawi village.* Arriving back in Homs from Palmyra Nick and I parted company with Mike who headed off on his own to return to Salt. I made arrangements to meet up with him again back in the UK in a month's time and let him know how we got on with the journey home. His interest lay not so much in what adventures we might have on the way but more in seeing whether the journey might actually be accomplished with just the £30 we each had left after our excursion to Cyprus in June! I was confident, for we already had the return tickets for the bus from Athens to London and we should almost certainly get that far given the low cost of living in Syria and Turkey.

---

* In 1982 the worst atrocity was to occur in Hama when the army under the orders of President Assad conducted a scorched earth policy against the town, massacring by some reports as many as 20,000 of its citizens.

My plan was to return to Aleppo and catch the train across Turkey which we knew was cheap (allow say £5) and which had the advantage of removing the need for any overnight accommodation. One night in Istanbul (say another £5) should allow us enough time to sort out a bus to Athens (say £10). This would leave about £10 for food and incidentals (tobacco). It was Sunday afternoon by the time our hitched ride dropped us off at the station in Aleppo and I went into the ticket office to enquire about tickets. It took me sometime to understand that I could buy a ticket but that the train would not be departing for three days! It seemed there was only one a week. With only the briefest of thoughts as to how the ticket clerk managed to retain a full-time job I went back outside and broke the bad news to Nick. This would mean an unscheduled overnight stop in town and a change of plan – already the budget looked in danger. Luckily we found what must have been the cheapest hotel in Aleppo. For under £1 we had a double room with beds. There was no glass in the windows and the door to our room did not shut, but in the circumstances I thought it just the ticket. That night as a precaution we balanced one rucksack on top of the other and leant them precariously against the door. It was just as well as sometime during the night someone did try to enter our room but our rudimentary booby trap gave us fair warning. In the morning we stocked up with bread and fruit and caught a local bus the 30 miles up to the border post at Bab al-Hawa. Catching a lift in a pickup the last mile to the Turkish control point we then began to look for a ride that might take us the 700 miles to Istanbul.

We were in luck and soon found two British lorries whose drivers agreed to take us. They warned us that they were planning to stop for the night fairly soon and then do the journey without a halt. We would have a chance for supper at our halt near Adana. This suited us fine and I settled into the comfortable passenger seat in my lorry leaving Nick for the first time with the luxury of his own transportation. The meal that evening was welcome. I thought it well worthwhile splashing out on a huge *shish kebab* and various side dishes for one never knew when or where the next meal might be found. With my hunger satisfied I wandered over to the petrol filling station to buy some cheap matches where the pump attendant tried to interest me in purchasing a flashy plastic lighter instead. I showed him my neat steel petrol lighter I'd picked up in Damascus to indicate I had no need of another then realised he was puzzled as to why I now needed matches. When I showed him I was out of lighter fuel he took the matches back off me and ushered me over to the pumps. When I realised what he was going to do I froze to the spot, the thimbleful of petrol I needed was going to come from one of the pumps. I let him fill it, but maintained a safe distance. It wasn't just that he spilled about a gallon of fuel over the forecourt; it was mainly that he performed the whole operation with a lighted cigarette hanging out of the corner of his mouth. That night I slept again on top of the canvas cover of a wagon. Remembering my night in Saudi when it snowed I was pleased that it was now the height of summer and I had no need of a sleeping bag. In the morning I realised my mistake. The lorry had parked beneath one of the garage forecourt lights and all the mosquitoes in southern Turkey had come to hold a party there and I was one itchy mass of bites.

The long drive up to Ankara was exciting. The roads were poor and offered numerous traps for the unwary, but the worst hazards were the Turkish lorries we encountered. My driver called them "Tonkas" as they did indeed look like children's toy trucks; they were much smaller than the juggernaut I was riding in and all seemed to be overloaded, so much so that their brakes were often ineffective. It was that, or they never maintained them... or both. The gorges we passed were filled with upturned and burned-out trucks. I thought that the Arab *servees-taxi* drivers were bad, but these were possibly the worst drivers I had seen. I could only assume that they were paid by the ton they transported as why else would anyone take such risks?

That night we crossed the Bosphorus Bridge in a convoy of heavy goods vehicles. My head was out of the cab window taking in the spectacle of the Istanbul night sky and absorbing the chaotic sounds of a blend of car horns and the evening's calls to prayer. I reflected that we were leaving Asia behind; crossing back into a more familiar western world of supermarkets, reliable electricity and European newspapers. Only now did it really dawn on me that the great adventure would soon be over and I would shortly be starting a course of full-time education in a bleak northern polytechnic.

We were dropped off at a camping site on the west of the city which was on the main international lorry route used by all long distance lorry drivers travelling through Turkey. It seemed like a great spot to wait for a good lift back to Athens as there were even decent toilets and a restaurant, although we could not afford to eat there. There were others waiting for lifts seemingly having no difficulty at all despite looking more like tramps than we did. There were people of all European nationalities heading west, some with just the sandals they stood up in. I wondered how they had survived, often sporting pony tails and shorts which would not have gone down well in Arab countries, but these travellers appeared to be returning from nearer to home having probably spent their summer on the sunny shores of southern Turkey and presented no competition for us as we were the only ones heading to Greece to use our return tickets on the bus home.

By the end of the second day of watching every lorry departing the site heading off towards Bulgaria I seriously wondered whether we should revise our route. Others were arriving from the city and catching a lift northwards in a matter of hours, while we used up our precious cash on water bottles and Mars bars while waiting for something that was heading west. Having learned that a Bulgarian visa could be purchased at the border my mind was made up, never mind the cost I was heading for the Iron Curtain! We both found a lift easily and were soon on our way again in another matching pair of British lorries. It was Friday and had we waited for the train in Aleppo we would probably only now be arriving in Istanbul, using this to argue with myself that I was still on schedule I felt justified in having to spend the £14 which was the extortionate cost of a Bulgarian transit visa. As we passed through Edirne, the former capital of the Ottoman Empire (named Hadrianopolis by the eponymous Roman emperor) I remembered from my school classics lessons that this was Thrace - the country that armies passed on through. I would have to do likewise; denied the opportunity to explore this relatively unspoiled city with its many mosques and monuments by the exigencies of hitch-hiking.

One of the problems of travelling across many borders on a small budget was what to do for money. Cash was good as it could readily be converted, but I had learned to my cost in Egypt that it was also dangerous to hold it. There was also another disadvantage in that one had to decide what denomination to hold and how much to change into the local currency. By this time I held what little cash I carried in Deutschmarks having exchanged my Jordanian Dinars with a lorry driver at the Turkish-Syrian border but I still kept one £20 travellers cheque issued by Grindlays Bank in reserve. Some currencies were strictly controlled such as the Bulgarian *Leva* and could not be obtained outside of the country concerned. I was anxious to change currency as infrequently as possible because before I'd even spent any of it each time I changed money my meagre stash would decrease in value due to the commission I was obliged to pay. To some extent I had managed to offset this by securing better than bank rates in the *souks* where black-market trades could be made.

At the Bulgarian passport control I proffered my £20 cheque with a confident smile which belied my thoughts. I was banking on this working as it was going to be tricky to get from here to Athens if it didn't. My smile was obviously ineffective and I was taken off to one of the administrative offices, hoping all the time that the lorry would not proceed quickly through customs and would wait to pick me up. I hadn't left my rucksack in the lorry cab, which worked both for and against me as I wasn't in danger of losing it, but the driver would be under no moral obligation to wait to hand it back to me. The border official was most friendly and showed some delight in pulling a large folder from the shelf containing photographs of hundreds of travellers cheques and quickly starting to leaf through looking for a match with my own. With a satisfied grunt he found an image of a £20 Grindlays Bank cheque, but what he had not noticed however was that the elephant rampant logo was facing in the opposite direction. Although mine was the genuine article I didn't think I would win an argument on the subject and I quickly pocketed the change in Bulgarian *Leva* which he proffered from his own wallet and went outside to join my driver. It occurred to me later as I was meticulously counting the money I had left in my wallet; the official had probably pocketed that cheque. I now had about £10 left in a mixture of *Deutschmarks* and *Leva* and hoped this would see me across Europe, although the latter would be of no use once I had left Bulgaria.

As we travelled up the grey tarmac road to Plovdiv on our way to Sophia through grey villages containing grey buildings, and overtook small grey cars driven by grey haired old men in charcoal grey mock-leather jackets matching the grey-fabric seats of their cars, I began to wonder if the communists had banned colour altogether along with most western European influences. That night we pulled into a lay-by and I gratefully accepting the spare bunk in the lorry's cab (it was the first mattress I had lain on since Aleppo five nights previously) I fell asleep instantly only to be woken a few minutes later by a local woman knocking on the cab's door and offering her services. It wasn't long after shooing her away that we were woken again, this time by a Bulgarian lorry driver who offered to sell us diesel for any foreign currency we had. Foreign currency was scarce, but diesel fuel was plentiful and cheap but could only be bought by foreigners in designated fuel stations in exchange for foreign currency - for which of course a very poor official exchange rate was offered. Consequently there was a thriving black market in foreign curren-cy which if exchanged for the local *Leva* could purchase vast amounts of fuel for comparatively little money and my driver was keen to fill his tanks with as much diesel as possible before leaving the country. However the rate on offer from this local driver was not acceptable and he did not buy any fuel. The man was most keen to do a trade however, and seeing my small tin of Nescafé coffee offered me a few gallons of fuel which I saw no reason to refuse. Once this had been safely siphoned into the lorry's main tank my driver paid me in *Deutschmarks*. I could see there was an opportunity here for a little arbitrage! Clearly my driver was an old hand at this game and sure enough it soon became clear why he had held onto his foreign currency. We shortly pulled off the main road onto a large area of wasteland near a rather squalid looking fuel station. Shortly Nick's lorry, which had been following some miles behind, pulled off the road too and came to a halt alongside us. Before long a cyclist emerged from behind the buildings and pedaled over, slipping quickly between the two vehicles. Our drivers opened their doors thus effectively concealing the cyclist from all eyes, and negotiations commenced. Nick and I watched in astonishment as huge bundles of notes were handed across. The transaction quickly done the cyclist disappeared and our lorries made their way over to the pumps. The drivers offered us the same exchange rate for our remaining *Leva* and then proceeded to fill their tanks with diesel, handing over huge rolls of local currency in payment to the man we had just seen on the bicycle. I had no idea of the Sterling/*Deutschmark* exchange rate but I had clearly improved my financial position immensely.

At the Kalotina border crossing we were required to make our way on foot and meet up with our drivers again on the Yugoslavian side. I was pleased to be leaving Bulgaria for I had never quite shaken off the feeling that we were out of place, a mild paranoia not helped by our shady dealings at the roadside. As I waited at the passport booth I noticed on the counter beside the policeman a folded newspaper displaying a large photograph of Princess Diana. Mildly curious I peered over to try and get a better look and was startled to find I was now staring through the glass down the barrel of a revolver not six inches from my face. Trying out my winning smile again I moved away and handed over my passport - I wasn't going to come back here in a hurry.

Our lifts took us only as far as Belgrade where we thanked our drivers and wandered into a transport cafe at a truck-stop on the bypass. Some friendly drivers loaned us a cab to sleep in and helped us find a lift for the next part of the journey. Here Nick and I parted company as I set off in a truck headed for Accrington driven by a very chatty Lancashireman. I was sure Nick would find a lift shortly, after all we were on the final leg and there was no need to stick together any longer. I was getting very hungry again by this time, having had no real opportunity to eat a meal since Adana in Turkey a week previously and not wanting to spend much money feeling sure I would need all I had left for the ferry across to England. I had been living on biscuits and fruit since just after leaving Syria. Somewhere near Graz in Austria we stopped for the night at a little *Gasthaus* run by a friend of my driver. What kind of a friend she was I'm not sure as throughout the journey he had been regaling me with stories of his wife who had been the "Bolsover Blonde" of 1970-something. Anyway, the Austrian ran a good restaurant and I had a huge plate of *Wiener schnitzel* with chips as well as the cab to myself that night.

We had to wait several hours at Salzburg airport for the haulage company to fly out the necessary paperwork to allow the lorry to proceed further with its journey. Apparently there was some limit on the number of trips one could make across Germany without paying more taxes or fees and this lorry had reached that limit. After the constant progress of the last few days sitting around at the airport all day was frustrating, particularly as I was now in a race with Nick – wherever he was. The papers eventually came through in the early evening and we immediately left Salzburg and motored through the night across Germany into Luxembourg and Belgium and just managed to catch the last ferry of the morning from Zeebrugge to Felixstowe. I had sufficient cash for a ticket and so had no need to lie concealed on the bunk until we were parked below deck, which had always been my contingency plan. By early evening I was standing on the quay side back in Suffolk. My driver could only offer me a lift up to the main A12 road as he was heading for the north via London and I needed to go in the opposite direction, but luckily I had met someone I knew from school on the ferry and they took me the final few miles to my home town and dropped me off outside my local pub. Only twenty-four hours before I had been standing in Salzburg.

As I staggered into the lounge bar with my rucksack, the scene only a few months before of the less than meticulous planning for my journey, I realised that a few of my old friends where huddled in a corner over their pints. "Has anyone seen Nick?" I called. "Not for months" was the reply. Good, I had beaten him back, and promptly celebrated by buying everyone a pint out of the cash I still had left in my wallet. Later I found that there was no-one in at home and as I had no house key I ended that day on yet another kindly person's floor.

AFTERWORD

La culture – a dit un moraliste oriental –
c'est ce qui reste dans l'esprit quand on a tout oublié

Édouard Herriot – Jadis: Avant la première guerre mondiale, 1948

I t was not until I finally settled back into life in England that I realised how much I had been cut off from my contemporaries and from what had been going on at home and in the rest of the world while I had been away. It is interesting to recount some of the important events that happened outside of the Middle East during this period.

1979

❖ Someone called Tim Martin established the first J D Wetherspoon pub

❖ Margaret Thatcher became Prime Minister

❖ Monty Python's "Life of Brian" was premiered

❖ The price of milk increased more than 10% to 15p a pint

❖ The official bank rate reached an all-time high of 17%.

❖ Anthony Blunt was named as the fourth man in the Cambridge Spy Ring

❖ Sony introduced the Walkman.

❖ Pink Floyd premiered their live version of "The Wall"

1980

❖ Terrorists seized the Iranian Embassy in London

❖ Radio Caroline pirate radio station sank

❖ UK Inflation rose to 21.8%

❖ British Leyland launched the Morris Ital and the Austin Metro

❖ It was revealed that US nuclear missiles are to be sited at Greenham Common

❖ The pre-decimal sixpence was withdrawn from circulation.

❖ J.R. was shot on the TV show Dallas

❖ John Lennon was murdered

1981

❖ Prince Charles married Lady Diana Spencer

❖ Race riots broke out in Brixton and Toxteth

❖ Peter Sutcliffe admitted he was the Yorkshire Ripper

❖ Britain won the Eurovision Song Contest with an entry from Bucks Fizz

- ❖ Ken Livingstone became leader of the GLC
- ❖ The first episode of the sitcom Only Fools and Horses was broadcast
- ❖ Ronald Reagan became US president
- ❖ The IBM Personal Computer was released.

Somehow I didn't feel too disappointed at missing most of them.

PHOTOGRAPHS

Suez Canal – Convoy through the Bitter Lakes

Jordan – Exploring Salt

Jordan – Holy Land Institute for the Deaf, Salt

Jordan – Shopping in Salt

Jordan – Picnic overlooking the Jordan Valley

Syria – Norias at Hama (just before the shooting)

Syria – The ruins at Palmyra

Syria – Central Damascus from the Grand Hotel

Israel – Lowering the flag for Yom Hazikaron, Jerusalem

Egypt – Towards Cairo, from the Great Pyramid of Cheops

Turkey – Dancing bears in Istanbul

U.A.E – The author arrives in Sharjah

U.A.E – Building dhows on the beach at Sharjah

Lebanon – Crossing the "Green Line", Beirut

Lebanon – The harbour, Tripoli

Austria – Pausing for refreshments on the way home

ACKNOWLEDGEMENTS

I am grateful to the following individuals who generously agreed to read drafts at various stages of the writing or who offered encouragement and comment.

Lavinia & Nicholas Maclean-Bristol, without whom there would have been nothing to write. Martin Fisher, who reminded me of the great generosity of the Arabs. Louise Coubrough, who caused me to visit Egypt - for which I shall always be grateful. Paul Cawley who was my first reader and who's positive encouragement spurred me to complete the task, and who's knowledge of early pop songs was invaluable. Jane McKenzie-Wynne, who came to the stories afresh and so offered most valuable encouragement. Thanks also for Henry Hanning's careful eye in spotting several grammatical and spelling mistakes. I must also acknowledge my mother; to whom I apologise for a dearth of correspondence at the time, but for whom the reading of this book will hopefully provide some compensation.

Most importantly; my thanks to Sarah Maddock who helped greatly with the editing, and who may now be able to share a little better an insight into the world in which I lived before we met and the lives of those with whom I shared many exciting times.

I should also acknowledge the part played by Eric Edis who proved that it is never too late to write an account of an adventure - especially if it was a good one.

Finally, I shall always be indebted to the Dutch Jesuit priest with the un-spellable name who came from Beirut and showed me how to extract the last drop of spirit from a bottle of *jonge jenever*.

BIBLIOGRAPHY

Bar-Siman-Tov, Yaacov, *Israel and the Peace Process 1977-1982 - In Search of Legitimacy for Peace.* New York: State University of New York Press, 1994

Feddon, Robin, *Syria and Lebanon.* London: John Murray, 1965

Fisk, Robert, *Pity the Nation - Lebanon at War.* Oxford: Oxford University Press, 1990

Fistere, Isobel & John, *Jordan The Holy Land.* Beirut: Middle East Export Press Inc., 1964

Fraser, T G, with Mango, Andrew & McNamara, Robert, *The Makers of the Modern Middle East.* London: Haus Publishing Ltd., 2011

Graham, Helga, *Arabian Time Machine - Self-Portrait of an Oil State.* London: William Heinemann Ltd, 1978

Huxley, Julian, *From an Antique Land - Ancient and Modern in the Middle East.* London: Max Parrish & Co, 1954

Jaschke, Richard, *English-Arabic Conversational Dictionary.* New York: Frederick Ungar Publishing Co., 1955

Lankester Harding, G, *The Antiquities of Jordan.* Jordan: Jordan Distribution Agency, 1979

Searle, Patrick, *Asad of Syria - The Struggle for the Middle East.* California: University of California Press, 1990

Showker, Kay, *Fodor's Jordan & The Holy Land.* London: Hodder & Stoughton, 1979

Sugarman, Aaron, *Fodor's Turkey.* New York: Fodor's Travel Publications Inc., 1993

INDEX